HOCKEY
CROSSWORDS

AMAZON REVIEWS
ARE APPRECIATED

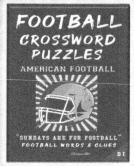  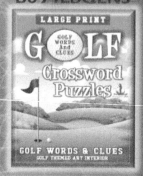

CLUE HELPERS

Abbr - Abbreviation
(short) - shortened word
"word" - Focus word, AKA, or quoted
pl - plural version of clue
sl - Singular version of clue
(slang) - Less known, slang or urban
( ) important clarification e.g. year

(3wd) # of words in answer
AKA - Also Known As
NN - Nick Name
___ - Fill in the blank
No Spaces in Mult. Word answer
UPPER CASE - Acronyms
USA and **UK/CAN** English

SOLUTIONS PG 104

Find an error? Email us: Designerinkbooks@gmail.com

Across

1. Sport___, Canadian broadcaster of NHL
5. Coaches helper (short)
9. NHL Canadiens G #34 Jake "A"
14. Avalanche ECHL affl Grizzlies
15. Fr. Flame "Thereon" Fleury AKA
16. NHL Blue Jackets C #38 "B" Jenner
17. Player's warm-up ride in locker room (short)
18. NHL Hurricanes D #77 "T" DeAngelo
19. A bad team does it often
20. Sellers of fake tickets
22. Prints the hockey scores (short)
23. Fr Bruin Carl Soderberg NN ___ Swede
25. "The Hockey Sweater" short story character
29. "A NHL year" of play AKA
34. Harvey the "H" of the Calgary Flames
35. Ret. Bruin G Tim Thomas NN
37. EHA = Elite Hockey ___ance
38. Fill a Jersey's sleeves
39. Panthers Patric Hornqvist NN
40. Ottawa Senators fan get togethers, Red ___ies
41. Player must dress, pre game arrival
42. HGH, for aging excuse
43. CGY Saddledome, became S___ bank in 2010
44. EDM Oilers were a "D" in the 1980s
46. Fr. Canuck C Jannik "H" AKA Honey Badger
47. Kings 1990s mascot Kingston, a Snow what?
50. Team did, for an elusive playoff birth
54. Player contract addition
59. Uniform after moth infestation
60. Coyotes share Arizona w the NFL C___nals
61. NYI 95-97 logo mocked as G___ns Fishsticks
62. Crowd sings ___ to anthem
63. Hockey HOF ind. 1963, (F) Shorty G___
64. American Hockey Coaches Association
65. Padding in a helmet, descriptor
66. TSN - That's Hockey hosted by Gino who?
67. Flyers G Carter Hart NN

Down

1. Devils alt. Cpt P.K. Subban NN
2. Senators play in the Atla___ Division
3. Br___way, when no D btwn player & goalie
4. Opponents AKA
5. At live game
6. 1933 Hart Trophy Winner, BOS
7. 12yr 7-team G Bob Essensa NN
8. "Story" movie said "Don't be a Hockey Puck"
9. A Baltimore WHA player, 1975
10. Uniform lace goes through this
11. Scored less than opponent
12. A G___al Manager deals w trades
13. Ottawa Senators 1st ever coach, Rick Bow___
21. Coaches wish star players came w one
22. Senators NN "P" Sens
24. NHL Kraken C #37 "Y" Gourde
25. Fits inside a hockey glove
26. NHL Lightning RW #10 "C" Perry
27. "H" Growth Hormone, a P.E.D.
28. Stanley Cup = 51.4K followers on "I" (short)
30. NHL Panthers D #5 "A" Ekblad
31. HOF Glen Sather's playing days NN
32. 14yr Capitals G, Olaf Kolzig NN
33. Ret. 10yr Hab Chris "N" AKA Knuckles
35. HOF Tony Esposito AKA
36. EA Sports NHL videogame series, visual
39. Dirty players are "H" by all, even teammates
43. Midway made the ar___ NHL Blitz game
45. No skate hockey, played sitting in a chassis
46. Was 1/2 the Czechmates w Jagr
48. Bruins intro song 1920s-1998
49. Winners names are, to the Stanley Cup
50. NHL Penguins D #2 "C" Ruhwedel
51. VAN Orca mascot let's smoke out of blow "H"
52. Rangers Don M___ey, 1984 All-Star MVP
53. Senators NN
55. NHL Islanders D #8 "N" Dobson
56. Detroit Roller Hockey Association
57. HOF Joe Sakic NN, Mr. Cl___
58. NHL pre-game tailgating entree
60. NHL & content - "All Rights Reserved"

PUZZLE 1

1	2	3	4		5	6	7	8		9	10	11	12	13
14					15					16				
17					18					19				
20				21					22					
				23				24						
25	26	27	28					29			30	31	32	33
34						35	36				37			
38					39						40			
41					42					43				
44				45					46					
				47			48	49						
50	51	52	53				54				55	56	57	58
59					60						61			
62					63						64			
65					66						67			

Hockey Fact: The National Hockey League (NHL) was founded on November 22, 1917. The league formed from much of the 1909 – 1917 NHA players and owners.

Across

1. 2002 Red Wings w Cup visited this President
5. NHL Kings RW #91 "C" Grundstrom
9. Blues alt Cpt Vladimir Tarasenko NN
14. OHL = ___rio Hockey League
15. Canucks logo, AKA whale
16. NHL Canadiens C #71 Jake "E"
17. 2008's Slap Shot 3: The Ju___ League
18. Hockey HOF ind. 1982, (C) Norm Ul___
19. They get your additional hockey tickets
20. Maple Leaf Gardens broadcast booth NN
22. NHL Blackhawks goal-song, "C" Dagger
24. HOF Frank McGee NN
25. "Highlight Of the Night" - Sports Center
26. 1990s Genesis, played hockey cartridges
27. Oilers used to share Edmonton w CFL "E"
32. HOF ind. 1963, (D) Didier "P" (CAN)
34. Blues D Torey Krug NN
35. Concession fountain offering
36. NHL Chicago Blackhawks State (short)
37. "Blue & Red" on a Rangers jersey
41. Players travel in it, from city to city
44. HOF ind. 1989, (G) Vladislav "T" (Rus)
46. Silver on an Avalanche uniform
47. AHL Cleveland Monsters on the scoreboard
48. A contract do-over
52. 3x Cup winner fr. G Andy Moog NN
56. 3 hours for an NHL game TV coverage
57. Pull goalie, put on what? attacker to tie score
58. Goalies keep puck from the net
60. Devils fans, Sec. 233 wear Triple D___ jerseys
61. Noise from a fan
62. Bruins Bill Gu___, 2001 NHL All-Star MVP
63. CHL = ___inental Hockey League
64. Game "shown" on TV
65. Team came up short
66. Stars share Dallas w the MLB R___rs

Down

1. Ret. 19yr Goalie R. Luongo NN = Bingo Bango "B" Luongo
2. Flyers share Philly w the MLS what?
3. NHL Golden Knights Captain Mark "S"
4. All-Star Skills Comp. event, "H" Shot
5. Degree place of future NHL stars
6. Blainville-Boisbriand's QMJHL hockey team
7. 1966 Flyers naming contest top prize = TV
8. Avalanche NN
9. Fr. Gretzky protector, Dave "S"
10. Try-outs are a player "E" situation (short)
11. Capitals share D.C. w the MLB what? NN
12. Common mid leg injury, MCL, ACL
13. HOF ind. 2020, (RW) Marián H___ (Slo)
21. HOF ind. 1982, (RW) Yvan Courn___
23. Sports-center occupation
28. Injured Reserve (status)
29. TV broadcasting, NHL's "M" revenue source
30. NHL, NHLPA C___ctive Bargaining Agreement
31. 80's great - Steven Donald Larmer
32. Condition of low value hockey card
33. Sec. 233 Devils fans wear Tr___ digit jerseys
35. % Abbr for statistics
38. Extra session of play: Abbr
39. 1947 Hart Trophy Winner, Rocket, MTL
40. Ticket at a discount, on what?
41. Game pucks are frozen to "P" bounce
42. Concession queue AKA
43. Star Spangled Banner sang pre game for "A"
45. NHL Coyotes RW #81 Phil "K"
46. NHL Maple Leafs D #23 "T" Dermott
49. Coyotes NN Biz's Wagon
50. HGH, is for anti what?
51. Capitals Head Coach Peter Lavio___
52. 1997 Selke Trophy Winner, BUF
53. NHL All-Star game, officially an ___bition
54. Fastest Ska___, All-Star Skills Comp. event
55. Fr. Flame Fleury, aboriginal heritage
59. 90's great - "Adam Robert Oates"

PUZZLE 2

1	2	3	4		5	6	7	8		9	10	11	12	13
14					15					16				
17					18					19				
20				21				22	23					
24								25						
			26					27			28	29	30	31
	32	33							34					
35												36		
37			38	39	40			41	42	43				
44					45		46							
			47				48				49	50	51	
52	53	54	55				56							
57					58	59			60					
61					62				63					
64					65				66					

Hockey Fact: The Rover position was the 6th skater on the ice, "roving" with no set position. The NHA (Pre NHL) did away with this position in 1911.

7

Across

1. A Hockey player in Montreal NN
5. Concession food, comes w sauce
10. Howi___ - very fast slap shot
14. New York Rangers' ___son Square Garden
15. Press consensus best NHL #45, Aaron "A"
16. TSN - That's Hockey hosted by Gino who?
17. Mascots fire them from air cannons
19. KY Derby winning horse 'Go For Gin' ___ from Stanley Cup, 1994
20. Canucks alt Cpt Brandon Sutter NN
21. AKA bleachers
22. Sharks share the SF Bay area w NBA "W"
24. Detroit AKA "Hockeytown" is a Registered Tr___ark
26. # of Nordiques Stanley Cups (French)
27. Trade talk, means team may "C" changes
31. 1909-18 NHA, prede___ of the NHL
35. EHA = ___ Hockey Alliance
36. CAN won this in gold at 2002 Olympics
38. 'Players do not take PEDs' - statement type
39. Hockey HOF ind. 1963, (D) Barney Sta___
40. Stanley Cup visited Late Night w "O'Brien"
41. Ticket at a discount AKA a ticket on "S"
42. NHL Senators LW #18 "T" Stützle
43. LAK '98 pick, 21st overall, Mathieu "B"
44. NHL Avalanche G #39 "P" Francouz
45. NHL Red Wings D #53 Moritz "S"
47. Penguins share Pittsburgh w NFL what?
49. Canucks logo, AKA whale
51. Penguins GM Ron H___ll
52. Pens Captain Sidney Crosby NN
56. Pittsburgh NHL player, 1925-30
60. Hockey HOF ind. '58, (D) Sprague Cleg___
61. NHL Islanders LW #27 Anders "L"
62. A Hamilton NHL player, 1920-25
63. Hockey HOF ind. 1992, (C) Marcel Di___
64. NHL Senators G #31 "A" Forsberg
66. HOF ind. 2010, (RW) Dino Ciccar___
67. Hockey HOF ind. 2015, (D) Chris Pro___
68. Puck face shape
69. Already "watched" game

Down

1. Broadcaster audio equipment need
2. NHL MVP award
3. Atlanta Gl___tors, Ottawa Sens ECHL affl
4. Fr Coyote LW Paul Bissonnette's NN
5. Puck played from one player to another
6. Sharks share SF Bay area w MLB OAK?
7. Hawks C Andrew "S" AKA The Mutt
8. NHL Devils LW #90 Tomas "T"
9. Star Spangled Banner sang for these teams
10. Early team travel method
11. Scoreboard display with no goals
12. Sergei F___ov, 1992 All-Star Fastest Skater
13. Rangers NN
18. Fr. G Eddie Belfour's NN, Crazy "E"
23. NHL film holder
25. HOF has teams, players, & ___abilia
27. Thousands needed to buy ticket
28. 14yr Capitals G, Olaf Kolzig NN
29. Fr. Shark, Pen, G Antii "N" AKA Nemo
30. CGY Saddledome had major ones in 1994
32. Bruins intro music "Cochise" by Audio___
33. NHL Hockey player in Edmonton
34. NHL film holders
37. NHL Predators D #57 "D" Fabbro
40. Puck shape
41. Rising "S", why Nordiques moved to COL
43. Hockey HOF ind. 1963, (D) Earl Sei___
44. VAN '82 1st rd pick, 11th overall Michel "P"
46. Fr ARZ Captain, player Shane Doan NN
48. The NHL did "get bigger" by 1 in 2021
50. CGY Saddledome went through one in 1994
52. Hockey HOF ind. 2016, (G) Rogie Va___
53. HOF ind. 1975, (RW) George Armst___
54. NHL Red Wings LW #73 Adam "E"
55. NHL Panthers C #27 "E" Luostarinen
57. Flyers share Philadelphia w NFL E___s
58. "Vision" to watch game
59. Bruins Bill Gu___, 2001 All-Star MVP
65. NHL Ottawa Senators Province: Abbr

PUZZLE 3

Hockey Fact: The Stanley Cup, first awarded in 1893, is the oldest existing trophy awarded to a pro sports franchise in North America.

Across

1. 1964 Lady Byng Trophy Winner, CHI
7. "Peter" Pocklington on Stanley Cup as? '84
12. Red Wings share DET w NFL "L"
13. CGY Saddledome went through one in '94
14. Ret. Leafs Cpt Dion Phaneuf NN Sloppy "S"
17. Popular team-store merchandise
18. Hockey player in Ottawa (short)
19. Roller Hockey Alliance
21. WHA Cincinnati Stingers logo
22. Puck crosses line just before 0:00 = buzzer?
26. Bruins NN "___ of the East"
28. Street for 'Red Mile' - Sens fans celebration
29. Sharks share San Jose w MLS "E" Quakes
30. "Happy"-ful fans. Also, TV show w dancing
31. All-Star game '98-2002, World vs North "A"
34. Anthem action
35. Jackets LW Gustav Nyquist NN
36. Goalies protect them
38. Ret. VAN G Kirk McLean play style
41. Uniform lace problem
42. SJS 2015 1st rd pick, 9th overall, Timo "M"
43. Knights alt. Cpt Alex Pietrangelo AKA
44. NHL Coyotes C #83 Jay "B"
45. NHL Bruins C #83 "K" Kuhlman
46. Saskatchewan Hockey Association
48. Mild contact of puck w stick
49. Orr's 1971 contract, 200K "P" year
50. Popular NHL sponsor type. Vroom-vroom
52. NHL's popularity in the 80's and 90's
55. 1972 WHA Miami team, moved to P___delphia before ever playing a game
56. Cold weather hockey, pick up games
57. They cheer after a goal
58. SJ Sharks D #61 "S" Hatakka

Down

2. Canadiens share MTL w CFL what? NN
3. EDM '97 1st rd pick, 14th overall Michel "R"
4. Bruins 1st owner Adams was a g___ magnate
5. Trade rumors, often ___ ymous
6. (Ret.) Markus Sten Näslund
8. Australian Roller Hockey
9. 15yr fr. Hawk Brent Seabrook NN
10. Hockey HOF ind. 1993, (D) Guy Lapo___
11. Did not win
15. NHL Leafs goal-song, "You Make my ___"
16. Ducks paid Kings $50M to "S" L.A. market
20. Bruins David P___nak, 2020 All-Star MVP
22. Team owner often does for public funding
23. NHL Flyers D #94 Ryan "E"
24. Represents a player
25. Even scoring AKA
26. Don "B" '92 All-Star Skills Breakaway (saves)
27. HOF G Ken Dryden NN
32. Thousands needed to buy ticket
33. A Toronto WHA player, 1973-76
35. Fr. Flame Fleury, Honarary Science Doctorate from "G" Ontario University
37. Hockey HOF ind. 1958, (C) Frank Foy___
39. Player must dress this way, pre game arrival
40. Number on scoreboard
43. 1974 Conn Smythe Trophy Winner, PHI
44. Bruins D Brandon Carlo NN
45. NHL Jets GM, "K" Cheveldayoff
46. Syracuse Crunch Hockey Club
47. Physical feature hidden under helmet
49. Professional Inline Hockey Association's
51. "Observed" the play
53. 90's great - "Ronald Scott Stevens"
54. Hockey HOF ind. 1970, (RW) Babe "D"

PUZZLE 4

Hockey Fact: The Montreal Canadians have won the Stanley Cup a record 24 times. This was the most by any pro franchise in NA until the Yankees won their 25th WS in 2009.

Across

1. NHL Blues LW #20 Brandon "S"
5. Name before Maple Leafs, 1919-27 (short)
11. 105mph slapshot - Al Iafrate AKA Wild "T"
12. (Ret) Leafs Cpt Dion "P" AKA Neufy
14. 1975 Lady Byng Trophy Winner, DET
15. 18yr Fr NHL G Tom "B" AKA Tomcat
16. Contract yeses
17. HOF ind. 2014, (G) Dominik H___ (Czech)
18. AHL Springfield Thunderbirds on scoreboard
19. CAN NHL TV show'er Sports ___
20. Canadiens Head Coach Dom Duch___
21. Masterson, only NHL player to have what? from on ice injury
22. NHL Wild's Training facility, ___ Rink
24. HOF ind. 2013, (D) Chris Che___ (US)
25. Hockey HOF ind. 1963, (F) Shorty G___
26. Canucks Brock Bo___, 2018 All-Star MVP
27. The Hockey News
28. NHL trading - of a player or ___
29. NHL film holder
31. Low scoring game is, to many fans
32. Jab opponent with stick blade AKA
34. "Pepper" what? player w speed, quickness
35. HOF ind. 1971, (LW) Gordon Rob___
39. Hockey movie 'Slapshot', actors AKA
40. (2021 F.A.) G Antti Niemi NN
41. 1970s Flyers NN, Broad St___ Bullies
42. Coast of Rangers, Islanders, Bruins
43. VAN Elias Pettersson NN
44. Expansion team entry payment
45. 90's great - "Tommy Mikael Salo"
46. 1990 Clancy Trophy Winner, EDM
47. NHL Flyers Captain "C" Giroux
50. A San Diego WHA Player, 1974-77
52. Fr. Canuck Jannik "H" AKA Honey Badger
53. Great players of old, complimentary title
54. St. Louis Blues ___prise Center, cap 19K
55. Win Stanley Cup, back to back years
56. Concession does for arena patrons

Down

1. Short handed goal (slang)
2. HOF ind. 2003, (C) Pat LaFont___ (US)
3. HOF ind. 2017, (RW) Teemu Sel___ (Fin)
4. 1990s Hockey VGs came on Catri___
5. Gatorade electrolytes prevent muscle "S"
6. # of Stanley Cups (physical objects)
7. Same "Stanley" named for Cup, in Vancouver
8. NHL Anaheim Ducks on the scoreboard
9. 1983 Adams Award Winner, CHI
10. Officials do it to unruly players
11. NHL Hamilton team 1920-1925
13. HOF ind. 1945, (D) Harvey Pul___
14. NHL Predators D #57 "D" Fabbro
15. Cleveland NHL player, 1976-78
20. Australian Ice Hockey League
21. Contract negotiator. Also, Vegas card giver
23. Police do with unruly fan at the game
24. Hockey HOF ind. 1974, (D) Art Cou___
25. 80's great - "Rodney Cory Langway"
28. '95-2010 sponsor, Canucks GM Place
30. 94 Ranger Olczyk, ok'd KY Derby horse to what? from Stanley Cup
31. Covers an arena
32. One who sells fake game tickets
33. "The Hockey Sweater" on CAN $5 bill
34. 1980's EDM Oilers owner "P" Pocklington
36. Negative contract reaction
37. HOF Ted Kennedy NN
38. Ret. Blue, Leaf Alexander "S" AKA Fixer
40. Latest arena built AKA
42. Sharks entrance song is by M___lica
43. "Honda" Center NN, Anaheim Ducks
46. Concession queue AKA
47. Bruins LW Jake DeBrusk NN
48. NHL Sharks C #18 "L" Pederson
49. Contract upping. Also, a poker term
51. Speaks for players (short)

PUZZLE 5

Hockey Fact: The most Stanley Cup wins of any U.S.-based NHL team is the Detroit Red Wings - having won it 11 times, as recently as 2008.

Across

1. 8-team, fr. G C. McElhinney 'spicy' NN
7. Worst place in the standings
11. Weekend game night (short)
12. Non playoff team's "course"
13. HOF ind. 2016, (RW) Sergei Mak___ (Rus)
14. Master Card ad (1997), "cost of conversation w son at hockey game?"
17. Hockey HOF ind. 1985, (G) Gerry Chee___
18. Avalanche share Colorado w the NBA N___ts
19. Statistic collected from gameplay AKA
20. ___mission = time mascot entertains crowd
22. Antler (type), spray used as steroid alternative
23. CAN NHL TV show'er Sports ___
24. Blues alt Cpt Vladimir Tarasenko NN
25. How to watch online NHL
28. Hockey HOF ind. 1958, (C) Duke K___
31. $ "offer" for players services
32. 90's great - "Adam Robert Oates"
33. Ligue Nord-Americaine re Hockey
34. NHL Islanders LW #27 Anders "L"
35. WPG 2014 1st rd pick, 9th overall, Nikolaj "E"
38. USHL = United ___ Hockey League
40. NHL Anaheim Ducks on the scoreboard
41. HOF ind. 2010, (C) Cammi Gra___ (US)
43. Australian Roller Hockey
44. 90's great - "Lawrence Thomas Murphy"
45. HOF ind. 2008, (C) Igor Lari___ (Rus)
46. Flyers James van Riemsdyk NN
50. NHL Lightning D #81 "E" Cernak
52. Season tix, holds that seat (short)
54. Juke & "J" around opponent
55. Ticket numbers $old counts as what?
57. Original 6 vs NHL-WHA merger "times"
59. Ottawa Senators logo, a R___ General
60. Hockey HOF ind. 1960, (D) Sylvio Ma___
61. Fr. 10yr RW "D.W." AKA Dutch Gretzky

Down

1. Hung on net for skills shot-accuracy
2. A Hamilton NHL player, 1920-25
3. Avg of NHL'er is 28
4. When team is exchanged for $$$
5. Laundered uniform status
6. Nintendo's 1988 "Blades ___"
7. Jaccob S___n won '20 All-Star Shot Accuracy
8. Bernie P___, left NHL for WHA year 1
9. Organizable stats AKA
10. 2015-17 "Hockey Wives" a reality what?
11. Late 80's Bud Light dog, sports advertising
15. Breakfast food eaten from Stanley Cup
16. HOF G Martin Brodeur NN = "S" Wallpaper
21. Hockey HOF ind. 1993, (C) Edgar Lap___
26. CGY Saddledome went through one in 1994
27. Hockey HOF ind. 1958, (G) Paddy "M"
29. NHL Devils LW #90 Tomas "T"
30. Ducks paid Kings $50M to? w L.A. market
35. 50-50 ticket prize depends on the # of
36. NHL Devils D #7 Dougie "H"
37. Hockey equip, when not in use
39. Joe Louis Arena AKA to Detroit natives
40. Eastern Conf. was Prince of W___, pre 1993
42. Draft qualifier e.g. 1st ___
47. Fr. Hawk C Dave Bolland NN
48. Wild Head Coach Dean "E"
49. A contract come-again
51. 1981 Lady Byng Trophy Winner, PIT
53. Fr. 14yr D, Ruslan "S" AKA Rusty
56. Martin Brodeur's 2003 popcorn spice damaged the Stanley Cup
58. NHL Flames C #23 "S" Monahan
62. 90's great - "Wayne Douglas Gretzky"

Across (continued)

63. Stick to a player, like a hammer to a carpenter
64. Currently have when out-scoring opponent
65. 1800s outdoor game pucks, frozen dung type
66. Sport___, Canadian broadcaster of NHL
67. 1980s EDM Oilers owner, Peter Pock___

PUZZLE 6

Hockey Fact: Not every player on the winning team is engraved onto the Stanley Cup. Only a select few players, coaches, staff, & owners are given the honor.

Across

1. NHL Islanders D #24 "S" Mayfield
6. Take Two Interactive, 2K "S" VG division, makes Hockey games
11. NHL Kraken LW #13 Brandon "T"
12. TOR AHL Marlies, play in ___-Cola Coliseum
14. Ottawa Senators logo, Roman Gen___
16. Ted G___, left NHL for WHA year 1
17. Common (sports) gambling term
18. Late 90s Sega ___rn console w Hockey VGs
19. A Oakland NHL player, 1967-76
21. Hockey HOF has 28_ players, as of 2020
22. HOF ind. 1989, (G) Vladislav Tre___ (Rus)
23. NHL Maple Leafs RW #24 "W" Simmonds
24. HOF has six__ On-Ice Officials, as of 2020
25. Hockey HOF ind. 1992, (C) Marcel Di___
26. Quit the game of hockey due to age
28. Arena sellers of merch
30. AHL San Diego Gulls on the scoreboard
31. Each one holds up the net's crossbar
33. Performance Enhancing Drug
34. Player scores 3 & fans will throw hats where?
37. 90's great - "Claude Percy Lemieux"
39. Coach's "strategy" AKA
40. Shutout, stat: Abbr
42. Don Cherry story "Keep Your ___ Kid"
45. NYR ECHL affl JAX team
47. NHL Canucks D #77 Brad "H"
48. Black 6oz disc
50. HOF ind. 1962, (LW) Sweeney Sch___
52. Hockey HOF ind. 1978, (G) Jacques Pl___
53. "Happy"-ful fans. Also, TV show w dancing
54. Sports Centre is filmed on one
55. Hockey HOF ind. 2015, (D) Chris Pro___
56. EHA = Elite Hockey ___ance
57. Sharks entrance song is by M___lica
58. 4 Cup winner Chris Kunitz NN
59. Hot cheese will, over top of concession nachos

60. Arena's concession's is air-born
61. Roch Carrier "wrote" 'The Hockey Sweater'
62. Fr Capitals G Jim "C" AKA Net Detective

Down

1. Concession soda tool
2. Detroit Red Wings Little "C" Arena, cap 20K
3. Fr Bruin Carl Soderberg NN = ___ Swede
4. The Flames are to the CGY Saddledome
5. "Hockey Wives" a reality what? show (short)
6. "Hockey Wives" show, a behind the "S" look
7. Hockey HOF ind. 1984, (G) Bernie P
8. Referees do, for the on-ice order
9. Anthem, best when a "T" singer performs
10. HOF G Martin Brodeur NN = "S" Wallpaper
12. NHL playoffs, a bracketed "C"
13. Cap Cpt Alex Ovechkin NN
15. NHL Predators C #11 "L" Kunin
20. Wild owner Craig "L"
27. Sutters Brent, Brian, Darryl, Duane, Rich, "R"
29. First games of the season AKA
32. Habs Joel Edmunson AKA Crop "T" King
35. Predators goal-song "___, I love it" (3wds)
36. Canadiens 1911-12 logo letters
37. NHL Blues' Training facility, ___ Community Ice Center
38. NHL Ducks D #29 Greg "P"
40. Hockey player in Ottawa
41. Don Cherry's playing career w Bruins
42. Jersey placement, on non game day
43. Exciting game AKA "bang ___"
44. Done to goalie for extra attacker
46. ANA 2006 1st rd pick, 19th overall, Mark "M"
47. Canuck twin, Henrik Sedin NN
49. Predators game, Sec 303 known as ___ block
51. Skills "R", an All-Star Skills Comp. event
60. On Gretzky's jersey, every team he played for

PUZZLE 7

1	2	3	4	5		6	7		8	9	10
11					12	13			14			15
16					17				18		
19			20	21				22		
23				24				25		
	26			27		28		29			
	30		31		32		33		
		34			35	36			
	37	38		39			40	41	
	42		43	44	45		46		
47			48	49		50		51
52			53		54		
55			56			57		
58			59		60		
	61				62		

Hockey Fact: Jaromir Jagr (Age 49) playing into his 50s? Since 1988 Jagr has played pro hockey. Known mostly for his time with Pittsburgh Penguins, Jagr has played 33 season, more than 2000 games for 9 NHL teams and 12 pro teams overall = the longest pro hockey career in history.

Across

1. Holds up arena roof
5. Needed after stinky arena beer
10. Concession beer servers
14. Marian H___, 2007 All-Star Shot Accuracy win
15. Kraken logo eye "red" color-name
16. WHA = World Hockey ___ciation
17. First game of season
19. Free agents want a bidding "battle"
20. Ha___ Brothers, chars. in 1977's Slap Shot
21. ESPN deal w JPN "K" Hockey VG maker
22. Ticket checker action w gun
24. Performance enhancers (slang)
26. Hockey HOF ind. 1985, (C) Jean Rat___
27. Streaming tech to watch hockey games
31. NHL Wild LW #17 "M" Foligno
35. A great goalie can "C" a weak team
36. Ret. 10yr Hab Chris "N" AKA Knuckles
38. NHL Ottawa Senators Province (short)
39. CGY Saddledome renamed to CAN Airl___ 1994
40. NHL Sharks Captain "L" Couture
41. OHL = ___rio Hockey League
42. NHL Anaheim Ducks on the scoreboard
43. 2x Cup win, Ret. Michal Rozsival NN
44. Leafs G Wayne Simmonds NN Wayne "T"
45. NHL Penguins D #58 Kris "L"
47. Coach chose not to coach anymore
49. Player is, for service to his team on-off ice
51. Spins w puck control, spin o what?
52. Coast for Rangers, Bruins, Islanders
56. The Flames are to the CGY Saddledome
60. Flyers full-length ___eralls pants, 1981-83
61. Jagr owns HC Klando of this league: Abbr
62. EDM Oilers to CGY Flames, esp. 1980s
63. SCHC = Syra___ Crunch Hockey Club
64. Every team has a "joker" AKA
66. Ret. 17yr Wing Henrik Zetterberg NN
67. Hockey HOF ind. 1974, (D) Art Cou___
68. NHL Predators Head Coach John "H"
69. Hockey HOF ind. 1963, (D) Harry Cam___

Down

1. HOF G Ken Dryden's "The Game" 1983
2. HOF Phil Esposito NN
3. A Ottawa NHL player (short)
4. NHL teams have General ones, for trades
5. QC Nordiques 1980's "M" Stastny
6. NHL Chicago Blackhawks State: Abbr
7. Recent happenings about hockey teams
8. "Small" amount detected in a drug test
9. NHL Coyotes D #86 Anton "S"
10. NHL Flyers C #58 "T" Laczynski
11. Bruins Head Coach, Bruce C___dy
12. HOF ind. 1963, (D) Bullet Joe Sim___
13. Anthem
18. 2013 Jennings Trophy Winner, CHI
23. Hockey HOF ind. 1965, (F) Fred Sca___
25. CGY Saddledome has major ones in 1994
27. An off___ regulates the game
28. 11yr North Star Lou "N" AKA Sweet Lou
29. Concession sweet AKA
30. Ret. Jet C Tim Stapleton NN
32. Stanley Cup visited Late Night w "O'Brien"
33. Loosen hockey skates
34. Patriots do for the anthem
37. An arena ice what? is 3/4 inch thick
40. NHL Sharks' Training facility, formerly ___ Ice Center
41. Put team together AKA
43. Hockey HOF ind. 1964, (G) Bill Du___
44. Like NFL, NHL games are always on one
46. The Hockey News is a what?
48. HOF G Martin Brodeur NN = "S" Wallpaper
50. Jets D Dylan DeMelo NN
52. 1990s NHL Breakway VG series by ___aim
53. Elimination Shoo___, All-Star Skills event
54. Scored less than opponent
55. Hockey HOF ind. 2016, (G) Rogie Va___
57. John T___es, '16 All-Star Shot Accuracy win
58. HOF ind. 2010, (C) Cammi Gra___ (US)
59. Bruins play in the A___tic Division
65. Team, refers to itself

PUZZLE 8

1	2	3	4		5	6	7	8	9		10	11	12	13
14					15						16			
17				18			19				20			
21							22			23				
			24			25		26						
27	28	29						30		31			32	33	34
35						36		37					38	
39						40						41		
42				43						44				
45			46				47		48					
			49			50		51						
52	53	54				55		56			57	58	59
60					61				62				
63					64			65			66			
67					68						69			

Hockey Fact: The desire of the NHL for a team salary cap led to the 2004-05 NHL lockout and cancellation of the Stanley Cup Playoffs for only the second time in NHL history (other = 1919)

Across

1. WHA version of the "Stanley" Cup (trophy)
5. Ontario Junior Hockey League
9. "Top" team, or top player AKA
13. Team tough-guy demeanor
14. CGY Saddledome had major ones in 1994
16. Ontario Minor Hockey Association
17. Each one holds up the net's crossbar
18. Mascot of the Nashville Predators
19. FL Panthers owner, Sunrise Sports & Enter___ment
20. NHL Kraken C #15 Riley
22. Stat column "organizing" AKA
24. A contract come-again
26. Former mascot of the Hartford Whalers
27. CGY Saddledome, to S___ bank in 2010
30. Flight for a busy, late travel team
32. Pads must shock "A" to prevent injury
34. Mascots fire t-shirts from "A" cannons
35. Down to Farm League
39. Capitals "Timothy Leif Oshie" (TJ)
40. Webbed glove of goalie, sometimes called a?
43. Fr Capitals G Jim Carey NN
44. Senators NN
46. 90's great - "Adam Robert Oates"
47. Kraken C Ryan Donato NN
49. Currently down in scoring
52. Worst teams are often the ___ popular
53. Full steam at net, for rebounds
55. Sabres NN
57. Hockey HOF ___, in the Builder category
59. Hockey HOF ind. 1965, (C) Ernie "R"
63. Hockey "arena" AKA
64. A Dallas NHL player
66. Hockey HOF has teams, players, ___rabilia
67. Stanley Cup originally for "Dominion Hockey Chall___ Cup"
68. AHL Ontario team
69. Ducks Teemu S___ne, 1998 All-Star MVP
70. Canucks Brock Bo___, 2018 All-Star MVP
71. Hockey HOF ind. 1972, (G) Hap Ho___
72. Tampa Bay NHL team NN

Down

1. Broadcaster audio equipment need (short)
2. Victor Erik Olof Hedman
3. Package of 12 pucks
4. AHL Reign location
5. Old school arena music player
6. NHL Blue Jackets C #38 Boone "J"
7. Hockey North America
8. Add to a team's negative column
9. Water sources on the bench
10. Contact teams through NHL.com
11. Cold weather hockey, pick up games
12. Pens alt. Cpt Kris Letang NN
15. "Cleaned" player after game
21. No-quit players have it
23. 1999 Clancy Trophy Winner, BUF
25. Great players, like objects used in war
27. Panthers NN
28. Hockey HOF ind. 1962, (C) Reg N___
29. HOF ind. 1994, (LW) Harry Wa___
31. Ticket sales do this after a series of losses
33. Fr. Enforcer Donald "B" AKA Brash
36. Br___way, no D btwn player & goalie
37. Hockey HOF ind. 2007, (C) Ron Fra___
38. Helmet collision mark
41. NHL Arizona Coyotes on the scoreboard
42. Steroid use is against it
45. Player who becomes lazy
48. TV's WKRP in Cincinnati character "Les" has WHA Stingers sticker
50. Caps RW T.J. Oshie NN
51. Fr. GM Place (Rogers) NN, VAN Canucks
53. Gifts containing minted player faces
54. Wild uniform red color name is Iron "R"
56. 2015 NHL Foundation Player Winner, SJS
57. Fr. Flame Fleury, aboriginal heritage
58. Hockey HOF ind. 1965, (C) Blair Ru___
60. NHL Predators RW #28 "E" Tolvanen
61. Hockey HOF ind. 1982, (C) Norm Ul___
62. NA Ice Rinks, 200 ft "L" x 85ft wide
65. NHL Senators LW #18 "T" Stützle

PUZZLE 9

1	2	3	4		5	6	7	8			9	10	11	12
13					14				15		16			
17					18						19			
20				21				22		23				
			24				25		26					
27	28	29				30		31						
32					33		34				35	36	37	38
39				40		41				42		43		
44			45		46				47		48			
			49	50				51		52				
	53	54					55		56					
57					58		59				60	61	62	
63					64		65				66			
67					68						69			
70					71						72			

Hockey Fact: For 21 seasons between 1980-2001 only 3 players had won the Art Ross Trophy for leading scorer – Gretzky (10), Lemieux (6) & Jagr (5).

Across

1. NHL Avalanche D #8 "C" Makar
5. Canadiens NN The "H"
9. Rangers NN
13. NHL Predators G #74 Juuse "S"
14. 1st black player in NHL, 1958
15. Currency type players are paid in
16. Flame Milan Lucic NN
17. YT, a streaming plat___ for hockey clips
18. ___sts make EA Sports NHL look good
19. A Oakland NHL player, 1967-76
20. Pavel Datsyuk Houdini-like NN, "M" Man
22. Known agitator player
23. Cardboard hockey stat display
24. 2012 Jennings Trophy Winner, STL
27. NHL Avalanche C #22 "S" Matteau
29. Surgeon-esque skill of camera guy
31. 90's great - "Owen Liam Nolan"
32. HOF ind. 2001, (RW) Mike "G" (CAN)
33. Final period
36. Dallas Stars American Air___ Center
37. Flyers G Carter Hart AKA "S" Hart
39. Public Address System
40. HOF ind. 1984, (C) Jacques "L" (CAN)
41. "The Hockey Sweater" short story character
45. EHA = ___ Hockey Alliance
46. "Spot" the arena is located AKA
48. Hockey HOF ind. 1997, (C) Bryan Trot___
50. The team "S" a lot to get the Free Agent
52. NHL Lightning D #44 Jan "R"
53. "Stat" collected from gameplay AKA
56. NYI '95-97 logo mocked as G___ns Fishsticks
57. Soda and beer found here
58. HOF ind. 2015, (C) Sergei Fed___ (Rus)
59. Betting term, starts with "O"
60. Nordiques uniform symbols, "fleur" what?
61. Bad team show type. Also, 70s game show
62. Oilers, most Nort___ of any NHL team
63. A Ottawa NHL player (short)

Down

1. 50-50 tix often supports local-city "C"
2. Police do with unruly fan at the game
3. WHA franchises, tended to "re" what, to new cities often
4. Eastern States Hockey League
5. NHL Blue Jackets C #15 Gregory "H"
6. A lion-like reaction of a fan
7. Fr Blues C Patrik Berglund NN
8. A step down pro version
9. Restricted Free-Agent
10. Modern NHL pro team travels in what?
11. General Admission Ticket
12. Team logo on fan's bumper
13. "Shot" type = hard w a windup
21. Fans do of their top hockey card
23. NHL affl., the AHL winner's "Cup"
25. Rangers Mike G___er, 1993 All-Star MVP
26. Hockey HOF ind. 2012, (C) Adam O___
28. "The Hockey Sweater" short story, decade
30. Lightning's St. Pete Times Forum NN, The Ice "P"
33. Ma___ Electronics = early NHL VG consoles
34. NHL Devils D #7 Dougie "H"
35. Penguins share Pittsburgh w MLB P___es
37. Wing D Nick Leddy NN
38. Practice squad player AKA
39. Don Cherry's suits, "repeat" look
42. Hockey Wives' show, top DL on "Apple"
43. NHL Jets C #18 Bryan "L"
44. Security do it with unruly fans
47. Pre 1926, Stanley Cup = "I" League comp.
49. Leafs share Toronto w NBA what? NN
51. 1995-95 Bruins Winnie the what? uniform
52. Hockey HOF ind. 1967, (G) Turk B___
54. 90's great - "Adam Robert Oates"
55. Kings mascot #"72" for LA's "A" temp (short)

PUZZLE 10

Hockey Fact: 1963 Champion Toronto Maple Leafs are engraved as "Leaes" on the Stanley Cup

Across

1. MLB Dodger mng. Las___ had MTL Canadiens mascot Youppi (then Expos) ejected

5. Hockey HOF ind. 2019, (D) Sergei Z___ (Rus)

9. NHL Panthers C #98 Maxim

14. Deke move objective vs opponent does what?

15. Canadiens 1911-12 uni, a barber "P" design

16. Ret. NYI Glenn Resch NN

17. The "F" in HHF, in DT Toronto

18. Fans pray to the hockey ones

19. Dustin Penner's 'breakfast' NN, Penn "C"

20. 2002 NHL All-Star MVP, Hawks "E.D."

22. NHL Blitz game can be found here

23. Star Spangled Banner sang pre game here

25. Roster play-able status

29. NHL Detroit Red Wings Little "C" Arena

34. Arena concession pizza division

35. Ticket x2

37. Ducks ECHL Affl. Tulsa O___oma Oilers

38. Mario Lemieux played while treated for Lymp___

39. Rabbit type food at concession

40. NHL Stars D #2 Hakanpaa

41. A Ottawa NHL player (short)

42. Flyers share Philadelphia w the P___ies

43. AHL Ontario team

44. NHL Capitals' Training facility, ___ Capitals Iceplex

46. 1980 Selke Trophy Winner, MTL

47. Fresh new leagues, described as "U"

50. Pro to call it quits

54. 1977 Slap Shot movie, Chiefs owner tanking team b/c of a tax what?

59. NHL Capitals C #20 Lars

60. Gary ___man, NHL Commissioner

61. The NHL maps each franchise their own "A"

62. 1980s US VG console maker w Hockey games

63. A lot of player memorabilia is counter___

64. Hockey HOF ind. 1965, (F) Arthur Far___

65. NHL Dallas Stars American Air___ Center

66. Hockey HOF ind. 1998, (C) Peter Sta___ (Slo)

67. Owner wants to get rid of team, action

Down

1. Paul C___y, 1991 All-Star Skills Fastest Skater

2. Loud lion-like noise from fan after a goal

3. ARI 2013 1st round pick, 12th overall, Max "D"

4. NHL Golden Knights D #23 Martinez

5. Exciting AKA "bang ___"

6. Arena drink type, always makes the game better

7. Father-time catches this player type

8. Devils LW Jimmy Vesey NN

9. Flander Fields poem by? is on MTL Canadiens dressing room wall

10. Amateur Hockey Association of Canada

11. NHL Rangers C #93 Zibanejad

12. Game pucks are "chilled", pre-game for game

13. Bruins alt Cpt Brad Marchand AKA "N" Face Killah

21. Stanley Cup visited "D" Letterman 1994

22. Trading - refers to a player or ___

24. An off___ regulates the game

25. Press consensus best NHL #45, Aaron "A"

26. Tight scoring game

27. The 1-timer was "T" perfectly

28. Don Cherry, 7 seasons w Rochester Amer___

30. NHL Hurricanes D #76 Brady

31. NHL Flyers Head Coach "A" Vigneault

32. Wild uniform red color name is Iron "R"

33. Cold weather hockey, pick up games

35. CBC's Battle of the Blades, this Figure Skate event type w Hockey players

36. Gordie Howe, most played NHL "star" games, 23

39. Players enter camp out of "S"

43. Hockey HOF ind. 1966, (D) Babe P___

45. NHL Oilers C #8 Kyle

46. "Rough-dirty" gameplay

48. Online support post for team

49. Sabres Rick M___, 1977 NHL All-Star MVP

50. 33rd pick 2005, James "___ Deal" Neal

51. NBA C___cs ran the NHL Bruins org. 1951-64

52. Bruins play in the A___tic Division

53. Sabres Daniel Br___, 2007 NHL All-Star MVP

55. Hawks share Chicago w the NFL B___

56. 1st black player in NHL, 1958

57. Fans, off the bandwagon after losses

58. NHL regular season start

60. 90's great - "Brendan Frederick Shanahan"

PUZZLE 11

1	2	3	4		5	6	7	8		9	10	11	12	13
14					15					16				
17					18					19				
20				21					22					
				23				24						
25	26	27	28					29			30	31	32	33
34						35	36				37			
38					39						40			
41					42					43				
44				45					46					
				47			48	49						
50	51	52	53			54					55	56	57	58
59					60						61			
62					63						64			
65					66						67			

Hockey Fact: WHA – World Hockey Association operated as a direct competitor to the NHL between 1972 – 79. In 1979 the NHL absorbed the WHA, adopting only 4 of the officially still existing 8 teams - Hartford Whalers, Edmonton Oilers, Winnipeg Jets & Quebec Nordiques. The remaining 4 teams folded in 1979.

Across

1. World Table Hockey Association
5. Mascots fire it from air cannons
9. NHL Golden Knights Captain Mark "S"
14. Gary "___man" Unger, 914 consecutive games
15. NHL Sabres RW #72 Thompson
16. NHL Flyers D #94 Ryan
17. TSN - That's Hockey hosted by Gino who?
18. Blackhawks camo jerseys on V___ans Day
19. NHL Blue Jackets LW #29 Patrik
20. Stanley Cup trustees "E" player names on Cup
22. A New York City NHL player
24. Ret. Hawk Kris Versteeg NN
25. NHL Kraken GM, "R" Francis
26. Hockey HOF ind. 1959, (LW) Cy Den___
27. 2000 Bill Masterson Trophy, NJD Ken "D"
32. Canes C Sebastian Aho's NN
34. Champion, back to back years
35. Blues Cpt Ryan O'Reilly NN
36. NJ Devils uniforms w green pants (short)
37. Sens share Ottawa w the CFL Red___
41. Sens C Chris Tierney NN. Hint: snake
44. They sit next to you at the game
46. Wrap your hockey stick with it
47. 90's great - "Stephen Antony Thomas"
48. Surgeon-esque skill of camera guy
52. Ret. 11yr C Mark "L" AKA Test Tube
56. 1980s EDM Oilers owner, Peter Pock___
57. 1980s US VG console maker w Hockey games
58. Gamblers make one on a game
60. NHL Capitals C #26 Nic "D"
61. Cleveland NHL player, 1976-78
62. Hockey HOF ind. 1967, (G) Turk B___
63. 1st black player in NHL, 1958
64. Term "Canuck" means Canadian, this way
65. Stick is to player, like a hammer to a carpenter
66. Color on the Bruins uniform

Down

1. TV camera connectors
2. NHL Bruins C #11 Frederic "T"
3. 1966 Vezina Trophy Winner, MTL
4. "A stadium" for hockey AKA
5. HOF ind. 2007, (D) Scott "S" (CAN)
6. Concession draft beer negative
7. Avg of NHL'er is 28
8. NHL Rangers Head Coach "G" Gallant
9. 1993 Calder Trophy Winner, WPG
10. Bruins play in the A___tic Division
11. Team F___no, 2015 All-Star Skills Relay win
12. Hockey HOF has 28_ players, as of 2020
13. Canucks Brock Bo___, 2018 All-Star MVP
21. Periods, eras or "A" in hockey
23. Lion-like noise from fans after a goal
28. VAN Elias Pettersson NN
29. Stanley Cup, rewarded every what?
30. ___mazoo Wings, Blue Jackets ECHL affl.
31. DAL 2000 1st round pick, 25th overall, Steve
32. EA Sports NHL makers, located in Burnaby British ___mbia
33. NHL Flames RW #15 "B" Richardson
35. 90's great - "Robert Bowlby Blake"
38. Sony PlayStation Hockey VG format: Abbr
39. Couples cam encourages it
40. Fan butt goes in one
41. D.C. NHL player
42. Goal in "unattended" net AKA
43. Fr Blues C Patrik Berglund NN
45. BOS 2003 1st rd pick, 21st overall, Mark "S"
46. Wings Affl, ECHL Walleye
49. A Toronto WHA player, 1973-76
50. Locker room clean-up tool
51. Game "completed"
52. PED testing places
53. Sharks entrance song is by M___lica
54. Blues alt Cpt Vladimir Tarasenko NN
55. Hockey HOF ind. 1963, (D) Harry Cam___
59. Negative, scary noise from a fan

PUZZLE 12

Hockey Fact: 1972 Champion Boston Bruins are engraved as "BQSTQN" on the Stanley Cup

Across

1. A roll AKA ___ of 50-50 tickets
5. Needed after stinky arena beer
10. NHL Blue Jackets D #22 Jake "B"
14. HOF ind. 2020, (RW) Marián H___ (Slo)
15. Kraken logo eye "red" (type, name)
16. EHA = Elite Hockey ___ance
17. First game of season AKA
19. Old arena roof, black covering
20. Future HOF Joe 'Jumbo' Thor___
21. ESPN had deal w JPN "K" Co., Hockey VG
22. Ticket checker action w gun
24. Team equipment AKA
26. Hockey HOF ind. 1985, (C) Jean Rat___
27. NHL on YT, streams
31. NHL Wild LW #17 Foligno
35. A great goalie can ___ a weak team
36. Ret. 10yr Hab Chris "N" AKA Knuckles
38. NHL Ottawa Senators Province (short)
39. CGY Saddledome renamed CAN Airl___ '94
40. NHL Sharks Captain "L" Couture
41. OHL = ___rio Hockey League
42. NHL Anaheim Ducks on the scoreboard
43. 2x Cup win, Ret. Michal Rozsival NN
44. Fr. Hawk, Jet Byfuglien NN = The 33 "T"
45. NHL Penguins D #58 Kris "L"
47. Coach chose not to coach anymore
49. Pro$ are ___ to play
51. Spins w puck control, spin o what?
52. A Division in the Eastern Conference
56. The Flames are to the CGY Saddledome
60. Ticket scanning gun noise
61. Jagr owns HC Klando of this league: Abbr
62. EDM Oilers to CGY Flames, esp. 1980s
63. NHL Red Wings LW #73 Adam "E"
64. Team joker AKA
66. Ret. 17yr Wing Henrik Zetterberg NN
67. A G___al Manager deals w trades
68. NHL Predators Head Coach John "H"
69. M. Berg___, QC Nordiques coach 1980-87

Down

1. 1st year player (short)
2. HOF Phil Esposito NN
3. A Ottawa NHL player (short)
4. NHL teams have General ones, for biz & trades
5. QC Nordiques 1980's Stastny
6. NHL Chicago Blackhawks State: Abbr
7. Goalies protect them
8. Possible amount detected in a drug test
9. NHL Coyotes D #86 Anton "S"
10. Star Spangled what?
11. NBA C___cs ran the Bruins org. 1951-64
12. Rangers Don M___ey, 1984 All-Star MVP,
13. Tampa Bay NHL team NN
18. 2013 Jennings Trophy Winner, CHI
23. Hockey HOF ind. 1965, (F) Fred Sca___
25. Calgary Flames Saddledome experienced major ones in 1994 (short)
27. An off___ regulates the game
28. 11yr North Star Lou "N" AKA Sweet Lou
29. Concession sweet AKA
30. Ret. Jet C Tim Stapleton NN
32. Stanley Cup visited Late Night w "O'Brien"
33. Loosen hockey skates
34. Patriots do for the anthem
37. An arena ice what? is 3/4 inch thick
40. NHL Sharks' Training facility, formerly ___ Ice Center
41. Put team together
43. Hockey HOF ind. 1964, (G) Bill Du___
44. Directly shoot a passed puck, a one what?
46. The Hockey News is a what?
48. HOF G Martin Brodeur NN ="S" Wallpaper
50. Jets D Dylan DeMelo NN
52. WHA Cincinnati Stingers logo
53. Damaged uniform
54. Hockey HOF ind. 1950, (C) Joe Ma___
55. Hockey HOF ind. 2016, (G) Rogie Va___
57. John T___es, 2016 All-Star Skills Shot Accuracy
58. HOF ind. 2010, (C) Cammi Gra___ (US)
59. Bruins play in the A___tic Division
65. Team, refers to itself

PUZZLE 13

¹	²	³	⁴	■	⁵	⁶	⁷	⁸	⁹	■	¹⁰	¹¹	¹²	¹³
¹⁴				■	¹⁵					■	¹⁶			
¹⁷			¹⁸			■	¹⁹			■	²⁰			
²¹					■	²²			²³				
■	■	²⁴		²⁵	■	²⁶				■	■
²⁷	²⁸	²⁹			³⁰	■	³¹		³²	³³	³⁴
³⁵				■	³⁶	³⁷		■	³⁸		
³⁹			⁴⁰				⁴¹			
⁴²		■	⁴³			■	⁴⁴			
⁴⁵		⁴⁶		■	⁴⁷	⁴⁸			
■	⁴⁹		⁵⁰	■	⁵¹			■
⁵²	⁵³	⁵⁴		⁵⁵	■	⁵⁶		⁵⁷	⁵⁸	⁵⁹
⁶⁰			■	⁶¹		⁶²			
⁶³			⁶⁴		⁶⁵	■	⁶⁶		
⁶⁷			⁶⁸			■	⁶⁹		

Hockey Fact: Wayne Douglas Gretzky is NHL's all-time leading goal scorer, assist producer & point total. Gretzky tallied more assists than any other player scored total points. He is the NHL's only player to total 200+ points in a single season, something he achieved 4 times.

Across

1. Place in NHL HQ, review game tapes
7. NHL Panthers C #98 "M" Mamin
12. NHL Bruins LW #56 Erik "H"
13. NHL, NHLPA Collective Bargaining A___ment
14. A Las Vegas NHL player
17. Hockey HOF ind. 1992, (LW) Woody Du___
18. (FA) Eric Craig Staal
19. EA Sports NHL series, "visual"
21. Contract agreement
22. Goalies blocker AKA what? pad
26. Arena climb obstacles
28. "The Hockey Sweater" in small town "R" QC
29. A player's best years
30. Hockey HOF ind. 2012, (C) Adam O___
31. Team's will "R" unneeded player(s)
34. Each one holds up the net's crossbar
35. NHL HQ located in "M" town Manhattan
36. 6-team fr. goalie Dwayne Roloson NN
38. NHL Kraken C #15 Riley "S"
41. Low scoring game is, to many fans
42. The team "S" a lot to get the Free Agent
43. Owner vs owner scoring competition
44. Toronto's team name before Maple Leafs, 1919-27 (short)
45. 1997 All-Star Skills Fastest Skater, Peter "B"
46. "Observed" the play
48. 80's great - "Steven Donald Larmer"
49. Ret. Pens C Maxime Talbot NN "M" Max
50. J Sakic, un___ited in Sandler's Happy Gilmore
52. Goalie "held" the puck
55. Top coach type
56. HOF G Ken Dryden AKA the 4-"S" Goalie
57. Arena nachos nutritional units (short)
58. BOS 1986 1st rd pick, 13th overall, Craig "J"

Down

2. Roller Hockey Alliance
3. ANA 2011 1st rd pick, 30th overall Rickard "R"
4. 6 "O" pucks are NHL regulation weight
5. Penguin Greg P___, 1973 NHL All-Star MVP
6. 90's great - "Michael Alfred Gartner"
8. 90's great - "Alexander Gennadevich Mogilny"
9. Injury images
10. Sabres Daniel Br___, 2007 All-Star MVP
11. Rangers share "New York" w MLB what?
15. Fan feeling toward rival team
16. "Behind" in score AKA
20. Game broadcast, takes about "3hrs"
22. Arena concession bread food
23. Pro players operate fancy ones
24. Substitute player's energy. Also, edible fruit
25. All-Star Skills Comp. event, "F" Skater
26. Fast action drill(s) type
27. HOF ind. 1966, (D) Ken "R" (CAN)
32. Kraken, inspired by giant Puget "S" Octopus
33. NHL Capitals C #20 Lars "E"
35. Where to keep a trophy
37. NHL Coyotes D #46 "I" Lyubushkin
39. 1975 NHL All-Star MVP, Penguin Syl "A"
40. Stars ECHL Affl. Idaho Steel___
43. Wooden sticks vs "today's" - plastic w foam
44. Slap Shot movie, Newman's language, a lot
45. Cleveland NHL player, 1976-78
46. Syracuse Crunch Hockey Club
47. NHL maps each franchise their own "A"
49. EA Sports hit VG '94 ___nt League Hockey
51. (Ret.) "Daniel Denis Boyle"
53. 90's great - "Curtis Shayne Joseph"
54. HOF ind. 1970, (RW) Babe "D" (CAN)

PUZZLE 14

Hockey Fact: 1996 champion Colorado Avalanche's Adam Deadmarsh's last name was miss-spelled "Deadmarch" on the Stanley Cup. This was later amended, making it the 1st correction on Lord Stanley's Cup.

Across

1. Soft, raised shot of puck
5. Canes Cpt Jordan Staal NN
11. Bruins ECHL affl. Mariners location
12. NHL stars at awards ceremony
14. Do with a game on the radio
15. 2008 Adams Award Winner, WSH
16. Erie's OHL hockey team
17. Convince a player to sign. Also, fishing object
18. Upper body injury area
19. "Guy" Lafleur, phonetically
20. Panthers NN
21. Goalie objective with puck
22. Peter F___erg, '98 All-Star Skills Shot Accuracy
24. Lightning share Tampa Bay w NFL what? NN
25. Washed-up player, AKA has ___
26. Sega ___rn console w Hockey VGs
27. (Ret.) Ryan James Kesler
28. Anthem instils this in fans
29. Fr 5-team G Johan Hedberg NN (string toy)
31. Player is, for service to team on-off ice
32. Leafs C Jason Spezza NN
34. Huge beer holder at sports bar
35. Famous TV award has "Sports" brand
39. Toronto WHA player, 1973-76
40. Canadiens 1911-12 uniform, barber "P" design
41. Opponents do this for loose puck
42. Nassau Veterans Memorial Coliseum, AKA ___oleum
43. Australian Ice Hockey League
44. 80's great - "Glenn Chris Anderson"
45. EA Sports NHL videogame series, "visual"
46. Midway - ___de NHL Blitz game
47. Arena climb obstacles
50. Blues Owner - Chairman Tom "S"
52. 18yr Fr NHL G Tom Barrasso, NN
53. Ottawa NHL player
54. On the back of a hockey jersey
55. Given to the greats at HOF
56. Blues Cpt Ryan O'Reilly NN

Down

1. All-Star Skills Comp. event, "F" Skater
2. Less filling arena beer option
3. Hockey HOF ind. 1945, (G) Charlie Gard___
4. Penguins NN
5. Fan noises after a ref's bad call
6. Avg NHL game event time is 3
7. Hockey HOF ind. 1950, (D) Newsy Lal___
8. Blues Cpt Ryan O'Reilly NN
9. Stick finish
10. Colorado Avalanche Cup win, time from QC relocation
11. ANA 2006 1st rd pick, 19th overall Mark "M"
13. Get rid of player salary. Also, place w garbage
14. Team IDs
15. Ottawa Senators primary Home color
20. Fr G great Curtis Joseph's NN
21. NHL Red Wings D #53 Moritz "S"
23. They exchange their $ for tickets
24. Fr G Ilya Bryzgalov NN
25. AHL Bridgeport Islanders on the scoreboard
28. Has sports writing on it
30. Ret. 7x All-Star, Sandis Ozolins NN
31. "Yank" the goalie AKA
32. Flyers G Carter Hart AKA "S" Hart
33. French CAN food eaten from Stanley Cup
34. NHL Coyotes LW #22 Larsson
36. HOF Mike Modano NN
37. Flanders Fields poem by? is on MTL dressing room wall
38. NYR alt Cpt Artemi Panarin NN
40. CBJ 2004 1st rd pick, 8th overall Alexandre "P"
42. NHL is a "M" market league, just big cities
43. Goalies pads are like a knights "A"
46. NHL Calgary Flames Province (short)
47. Spangled Banner
48. NHL Hurricanes D #77 "T" DeAngelo
49. Hockey HOF ind. 1990, (D) Fernie Fl___
51. Game streaming problem

PUZZLE 15

Hockey Fact: In 1972 the average NHL player salary was $25,000 USD. Contrast to today's average salary being a whopping 2.55M USD. Today's highest paid player is Auston Matthews at $15.9M while 161 players make the league minimum of $700,000.

Across

1. Predators NN Dorktown "C"
7. Sami K___en, 2000 All-Star Skills Fastest Skater
11. Not-so-good player
12. Rodents found in old arenas
13. Hawks wear Camof___ jerseys - Veterans Day
14. 2008 NHL All-Star MVP, Canes "E.S."
17. NHL Stars D #4 "M" Heiskanen
18. NHL Edmonton Oilers Province (short)
19. NHL-NHLPA Collective B___ining Agreement
20. Bernie P___, left NHL for WHA year 1
22. 4 Cup winner Chris Kunitz NN
23. To give a player a nickname
24. Owner wants to get rid of team, action
25. Holds jocks onto players
28. Br___way, no D btwn player(s) & goalie
31. Good seats can ___ all the action
32. NHL Islanders LW #28 Michael "D"
33. Sport___, Canadian broadcaster of NHL
34. AHL Toronto Marlies on the scoreboard
35. 10yr fr. ATL WPG Jim "S" AKA Slats
38. LAK 1986 1st rd pick, 2nd overall, Jimmy "C"
40. Elite Hockey Alliance
41. NHL Rangers G #31 "I" Shesterkin
43. Skate tighten action
44. Coaches tell team to take one for cardio
45. Shawn H___ff, 2008 NHL All-Star Skills Fastest Skater
46. Gatorade electrolytes prevent muscle ___
50. NHL Penguins D #58 "K" Letang
52. 90's great - "Kirk Alan McLean"
54. Check NHL.com for one (short)
55. The team "S" a lot to get the Free Agent
57. NHL Lightning D #81 "E" Cernak
59. Hurricanes share N. Carolina w NBA H___ts
60. Penguins share Pittsburgh w MLB P___es
61. Arena ice is set at what? celsius
63. Hockey HOF ind. 2002, (C) Bernie Fed___
64. Goal limit per period
65. NHL Oilers GM, "K" Holland
66. Already watched game
67. Fr. Devils RW David Clarkson NN = Grit "G"

Down

1. Arena car hold
2. Sports writer's boss
3. 90's great - "Tommy Mikael Salo"
4. EDM 1999 1st rd pick, 13th overall, Jani "R"
5. Trading - of "a player" or ___
6. MTL mascot Youppi, 1st to switch what?
7. Avs owners also own W___rt dept stores
8. CBC's Battle of the Blades, Figure Skating w Hockey players - event type
9. Player signs = ___ play for e.g. 1M this year
10. Oiler alt. Cpt Leon Draisaitl NN
11. Mocks opponent, bird slang
15. Country the Detroit Cougars played their 1st NHL season
16. NHL Sharks RW #62 Kevin "L"
21. Hockey HOF ind. 1989, (C) Darryl Sit___
26. Knights LW Max Pacioretty AKA "P" Ready
27. Ret. 600g now Czech politician, Jiri "S" AKA Guma
29. Hockey HOF ind. 1958, (C) Duke "K"
30. Travelling team is on one
35. Pros sign cards & posters with them
36. NHL Capitals C #29 Hendrix "L"
37. Don Cherry's ___ Sock'em video series
39. NHL "year" of play AKA
40. Oilers share Edmonton w the CFL what?
42. Lion-like noise heard from fans after a goal
47. Why NHL Hamilton Tigers folded 1925
48. Don Cherry, outspoken, describes his what?
49. Ret. Blue, Leaf Alexander "S" AKA Fixer
51. Fr. Blues G, S. Cup champ Jake Allen's NN
53. 2m penalty
56. Hockey HOF ind. 1958, (D) Red Du___
58. 4 Cup winner Chris Kunitz NN
62. Hockey player in Ottawa (short)

PUZZLE 16

Hockey Fact: HOF Dickie Moore, a member of 6 Stanley Cup wining teams, has had his name spelled differently 5 times - Richard Moore, D. Moore, R. Moore, Rich Moore, Dickie Moore.

Across

1. EA Sports NHL makers, located in Burnaby ___ish Columbia
5. E"A" Sports NHL video game publisher
9. NHL Devils G #41 "S" Wedgewood
14. HOF ind. 1982, (RW) Yvan Courn___
15. NHL Senators D #98 Victor "M"
16. Bruins intro song 1920s-1998
17. NHL Sharks LW #94 Alexander "B"
19. A Oakland NHL player, 1967-76
20. Matching player trade (3wd)
21. Jaws ___ is heard during Sharks PP
22. Late in the week game night (short)
23. Stanley Cup Playoffs happen per a___
25. They get your additional hockey tickets
29. NHL Flyers Captain "C" Giroux
33. NHL Blue Jackets LW #50 Robinson
34. Ottawa Senators logo, Roman Gen___
36. Taunt goalie AKA
37. NHL Kraken GM, "R" Francis
38. Sharks G James Reimer NN = Magic Angel "R" from Winnipeg
40. Totals (short)
41. NHL awards ceremonies take place per?
44. VAN Elias Pettersson NN
45. NHL Stars D #4 "M" Heiskanen
46. NHL Hurricanes C #18 Derek "S"
48. Fans pics taken w players
50. Hockey HOF ind. 2016, (C) Eric Lin___
52. 94 Ranger Olczyk, ok'd KY Derby horse to what? from Stanley Cup
53. Final scores, added up
56. 2008 NHL All-Star MVP, Canes "E.S."
62. NHL Hurricanes G #32 "A" Raanta
63. Kraken C Ryan Donato NN
64. Ret. Blue & Leaf Alexander "S" AKA Fixer
65. Sabres share Buffalo w the NFL B___
66. Future HOF Joe 'Jumbo' Thor___
67. Fr. QC Nordiques NN
68. NHL Player must dress, pre game arrival
69. Did perform anthem

Down

1. 17yr G Don Beaupre's NN
2. ANA 2005 2nd overall pick, Bobby "R"
3. Sabres Daniel Br___, 2007 All-Star MVP
4. Ret. Leafs Cpt D. Phaneuf NN = "T" Cone
5. A San Diego WHA Player, 1974-77
6. CGY Saddledome went through one in '94
7. Hockey HOF ind. 1958, (D) Red Du___
8. Canadian teams in the NHL
9. 16yr C Valtteri Filppula NN
10. Last active player from Original Six era, '83
11. 1st black player in NHL, 1958
12. NHL "franchise" AKA
13. "Vision" to watch game
18. Uneventful game, descriptor
24. NHL Carolina Hurricanes State: Abbr
25. Rocket's chipped teeth, caused by drinking from Stanley 1957
26. 2018 Vezina Trophy Winner, NSH
27. Refs do w puck at faceoffs
28. Sabres NN
30. "Loosen" hockey skates
31. Arena entrances
32. Detroit's NN, Hock___wn
33. Modern and pre-modern pro hockey "E"
35. Hockey HOF ind. 1975, (D) Pierre Pi___
39. NHL on TV
42. After refreshing NHL.com
43. Panthers share Miami w the MLB what?
45. Avs C Nazem Kadri AKA Nifty "M"
47. Shortened / Abbr for "number" (for stats)
49. Slapshots over 100 mph, considered what?
51. 2011 Ted Lindsay Award winner, VAN
53. 1980's QC Nordiques Marian, Anton & Peter S___y
54. Player names are engraved ___ Stanley Cup
55. Flames Head Coach Darryl Su___
57. "Player" type, e.g. position. Also, actors "part"
58. Hockey HOF ind. 2020, (RW) Jarome Ig___
59. NHL Calgary Flames Province (short)
60. Rangers Don M___ey, 1984 All-Star MVP
61. 1972-74 WHA L.A. Sharks, played part-time at "L" Beach arena

PUZZLE 17

Hockey Fact: There are 3 Physical Stanley Cups – 1 is the original bowl of the Dominion Hockey Challenge Cup, 2 is the authentic "Presentation Cup", and 3 is the spell-corrected "Permanent Cup" on display at the Hockey Hall of Fame.

Across

1. "The Hockey Sweater", story & short what?
5. 2020 Clancy Trophy Winner, MIN
10. Apply a number to a player's skill
14. OHL = ___rio Hockey League
15. Gerry Che___, left NHL for WHA year 1
16. HOF ind. 1971, (LW) Gordon Rob___
17. NHL Panthers D #52 MacKenzie "W"
19. 90's great - "Stephen Antony Thomas"
20. HOF ind. 1989, (G) Vladislav Tre___ (Rus)
21. "Oh say can you see….."
22. Many NHLers have super___, rituals
24. O___us are thrown on the ice at Wings games
26. Hockey HOF ind. 2001, (RW) Mike Gar___
27. HOF ind. 2008, (C) Igor "L" (Rus)
31. Concession pizza, lots of oily "G"
35. A lion-like reaction from a fan after a goal
36. "Hockey Wives" reality TV, a look at the "L" of player's Mrs.
38. Russian Hockey League
39. NHL Blue Jackets D #22 Jake "B"
40. Place a "bet" on the game AKA
41. NHL Blues LW #81 James "N"
42. NHL All-Star game, time in January
43. NHL Devils D #83 "J" Christian
44. 2021 Clancy Trophy Winner, NSH
45. Games we didn't win
47. Object collects ticket revenue
49. NHL Panthers C #27 "E" Luostarinen
51. Struggling goalie gets it mid-game
52. Fr. Flame Fleury's business after hockey
56. NHL Rangers RW #75 Ryan "R"
60. Panthers used to share Miami w MLS F___n
61. $ offer for players services
62. EDM 1993 1st round pick, 7th overall, Jason
63. Hockey HOF ind. 1959, (G) Tiny Thom___
64. Puck across 2 lines to Def. zone, no touch
66. EHL = ___ Hockey League
67. Derek ___erson, left NHL for WHA yr 1
68. 11yr North Star Lou "N" AKA Sweet Lou
69. Hockey HOF ind. 1970, (D) Tom Joh___

Down

1. Ducks NN
2. Hockey HOF ind. 1992, (LW) Bob Ga___
3. Devils a___nate uniforms have green pants
4. Leafs alt Cpt Mitch Marner NN
5. Derek San___, left NHL for WHA yr 1
6. Hockey cards are not ___ light resistant
7. HOF Mark Messier NN
8. NHL Devils LW #63 Jesper
9. A Cincinnati WHA player, 1975-79
10. Quit the game of hockey because of age
11. OHL = Ont___ Hockey League
12. Hockey HOF ind. 1963, (D) Jack Ru___
13. Oilers used to share EDM w CFL what? NN
18. Anthem singer if they are a TV celebrity
23. Hockey HOF ind. 1969, (G) Roy Wor___
25. Louie the blue ___ bear, mascot of the Pittsburgh Penguins
27. Seen inside neck of jersey
28. CGY Saddledome went through one in 1994
29. Connects opposing team's cities
30. HGH use by player, said to revive "V"
32. Bernie P___, left NHL for WHA yr 1
33. NHL Senators C #12 "S" Pinto
34. NHL Capitals C #20 Lars "E"
37. Devils LW Jimmy "V" AKA Ves (Vees)
40. Arena garbage holder
41. Fr. Star, Pen, Cap Matt "N" AKA Nisky
43. Angered fan response
44. HOF ind. 1962, (LW) Sweeney Sch___
46. Middle period
48. Arena car hold, usually covered
50. Devils AHL Comets city
52. Concession liquid holders
53. HOF ind. 2020, (RW) Marián H___ (Slo)
54. Stanley Cup originally for "Domi___ Hockey Challenge Cup"
55. Daniel S___, won 2011 All-Star Shot Accuracy
57. QC Nordiques Rendez "V" vs Soviets All-star game 1987
58. Devils, part of the M___politan Division
59. Hockey HOF ind. 1958, (C) Frank Foy___
65. "NickName" e.g. of team, players: Abbr

PUZZLE 18

1	2	3	4	■	5	6	7	8	9	■	10	11	12	13
14				■	15					■	16			
17			18			■	19			■	20			
21						■	22		23					
■			24		25	■	26				■			
27	28	29				30	■	31			32	33	34	
35				■	36		37			■	38			
39				■	40				■	41				
42			■	43			■	44						
45			46			■	47		48					
■			49		50	■	51				■			
52	53	54			55	■	56			57	58	59		
60			■	61			■	62						
63				64		65	■	66						
67				68			■	69						

Hockey Fact: The NHL does not actually own the Stanley Cup but uses it by contract with its two Canadian trustees

Across

1. $ listed on a ticket
5. 1-for-1 player trade
9. Puck from one player to another
13. VAN Orca mascot let's smoke out of blow "H"
14. NHL Lightning LW #18 Ondrej
16. Hockey HOF ind. 1993, (D) Guy Lapo___
17. NHL ___ ing Night, October
18. 14yr Cap G, Olaf Kolzig NN
19. NHL Blackhawks GM, "S" Bowman
20. NHL Rangers city
22. Leafs share Toronto w the NBA what?
24. FL Panthers owner, Sunrise Sports & ___tainment
26. Red Wings share DET w the NFL what?
27. Concession sweet AKA
30. Describes a team with a winless record
32. CBJ 2012 1st round pick, 2nd overall, Ryan
34. Players do not take PEDs
35. Leafs and Marlies (AHL) city
39. Back up position player (short)
40. NHL Canucks D #5 Tucker
43. 1948 Stanley Cup Champion Coach, TOR
44. Ottawa Senators 1st ever coach, Rick Bow___
46. Player, team outfit (short)
47. Watch hockey on the go from it
49. Hockey HOF ind. 1984, (G) Bernie P
52. "Leafs" misspelling on Stanley Cup 1963
53. Top of arena beer
55. NHL Sharks' Training facility, ___4America Ice
57. 1973 WHA NJ Knight's odd ice surface
59. 13 of these teams per band on Stanley Cup
63. Popular team-store merchandise
64. NHL Senators D #2 Zub
66. Scott N___rmayer, 1998 All-Star Skills Fastest Skater
67. Panthers used to share Miami w the MLS F___n
68. Ret. 14yr George Laraque NN
69. Bruins Bill Gu___, 2001 NHL All-Star MVP
70. Ret. enforcer Chris Thorburn NN
71. Known agitator player
72. CGY Saddledome went through one in 1994

Down

1. Hockey HOF ind. 2016, (G) Rogie Va___
2. Flyers full-length C___ralls pants, 1981-83
3. ___ foot, kicking out opp. skates so they fall
4. Bobby Hull's $2.75M WHA contract
5. Slap Shot, a "S" Comedy movie
6. Hockey HOF ind. 1960, (C) Jack W
7. "Entire" roster list
8. Ticket x2
9. Red Wings share DET w the NBA what?
10. NHL Stars G #35 Khudobin
11. NHL team in Dallas
12. Senators NN
15. Sharks NN
21. Soda and beer found here
23. Concession baked goods
25. 1951 Vezina Trophy Winner, TOR
27. Gary Bet___, NHL Commissioner
28. NHL law
29. Hockey HOF ind. 1971, (LW) Gordon Rob___
31. NHL Senators LW #18 Stützle
33. Don Cherry story "Keep ___ Up Kid"
36. Atlanta Gl___tors, Ottawa Sens ECHL affl
37. Pro hockey participant
38. Used to watch a game
41. NHL Washington Capitals Capital "O" arena, cap 19K
42. Owen "N", drafted 1990 by QC Nordiques
45. Arena brander AKA
48. LAK 2006 1st round pick, 11th overall, Jonathan
50. Attempts (short)
51. Waved by fans, especially during playoffs
53. Fr. Duck, Jet Teemu Selanne the Finnish "F"
54. Stat measurement
56. Concession rule, usually 2-beer
57. Zero goals allowed, a ___out
58. Refs do w puck at faceoffs
60. Sabres Daniel Br___, 2007 NHL All-Star MVP
61. Hockey HOF ind. 2012, (C) Mats Su___
62. Pens alt Cpt Evgeni Malkin NN
65. Early week game night (short)

PUZZLE 19

1	2	3	4		5	6	7	8		9	10	11	12
13					14				15	16			
17					18					19			
20				21			22		23				
			24			25		26					
27	28	29				30		31					
32					33		34				35	36	37	38
39				40		41				42		43	
44			45		46				47		48		
			49	50				51		52			
	53	54					55		56				
57					58		59				60	61	62
63					64		65			66			
67					68					69			
70					71					72			

Hockey Fact: The WHA, 1970's competitor to the NHL, signed away Fr. Chicago Black Hawks star Bobby Hull, for a 10-year, $2.7M contract w the Winnipeg Jets. At the time, this was the largest contract in hockey history.

Across

1. CGY Saddledome's $98M in 1983
5. Arena concession offering
9. CBJ, "electric" band heard after goals
13. Sharks Alt. Cpt, Brent Burns NN Chew___
14. Shawn H___ff, 2008 All-Star Fastest Skater
15. 3D Art software for EA Sports NHL series
16. NHL Coyotes D #86 "A" Stralman
17. Sergei F___ov, 1992 All-Star Fastest Skater
18. Jon Co___, Tampa Bay Lightning Head Coach
19. Lion-like noises from fans after a goal
20. Gordie Howe passed his hockey ones to Mark Howe
22. Tough break, major injury
23. Oilers, most Nort___ of any NHL team
24. Fans will after the game ends
27. NHL Coyotes RW #81 Phil "K"
29. NHL Predators RW #25 Mathieu "O"
31. Fr Leaf "T" Domi AKA Albanian Assassin
32. DET 1987 1st rd pick, 11th overall Yves "R"
33. Cleveland NHL player, 1976-78
36. CGY's Saddledome & VAN's Roger's Place
37. Stanley Cup is highly "D" among NHLers
39. 90's great - "Cameron Michael Neely"
40. NHL Coyotes LW #26 "A" Roussel
41. Given to the greats at HOF
45. Devils alte___ uniforms have green pants
46. Ret. enforcer Chris Thorburn NN
48. Tailgating purpose, besides beer
50. NHL Predators G #74 Juuse "S"
52. NHL Kraken C #37 "Y" Gourde
53. NHL Lightning D #81 "E" Cernak
56. Red Wings share DET w NFL L___
57. NHL Flyers Head Coach "A" Vigneault
58. Fan noise level during exciting game
59. Minor Leaguer's ___ the bus
60. NHL Sharks D #51 Radim "S"
61. M. Lemieux played while treated for ___homa

62. Acceptable shortened name for "stadium"
63. Back part of hockey skate

Down

1. Slang of the slang term Canuck (CDN)
2. Oilers 2011-16 cheer team name
3. Check NHL.com for them nightly
4. Krakens Brandon Tanev NN
5. NHL Oilers LW #37 Warren "F"
6. Stanley Cup tickets, action from an app
7. NHL Penguins LW #10 Drew "O"
8. 1987 'Hat Trick' game on the Commo___ 64
9. Alexander Mikhailovich Ovechkin
10. 10yr Habs Cpt Saku Koivu NN
11. HOF ind. 1970, (RW) Babe "D" (CAN)
12. NHL Penguins C #77 Jeff "C"
13. Wire type protecting arena in rough area
21. Done to Lacrosse balls to make pucks, 1800s
23. NHL Penguins LW #43 Danton "H"
25. Canadiens GM Mark Berg___
26. Devils Jimmy "Ves" Vesey, pronounced?
28. Press "articles" AKA
30. Press consensus best NHL #28, Steve "L"
33. Jamie "B" won '12 All-Star Shot Accuracy
34. "An arena" for hockey AKA
35. Violent fans do this after a Cup loss
37. NHL Oilers D #25 "D" Nurse
38. NHL Red Wings city
39. Buffalo's logo, 2 sabres "configuration"
42. Tampa Bay Lightning arena, cap 19K
43. From Nordiques to Avalanche, 1995
44. Fr. Canuck twin "D" Sedin
47. Anaheim Ducks "H" Center, cap 17K
49. Hypertext on NHL.com AKA
51. Game "appears" on TV
52. Senators 1st ever draft pick, Alexei ___in
54. G - 2x Cup wins w Avs, 2x w Canadiens
55. 90's great - "Keith David Primeau"

PUZZLE 20

Hockey Fact: 13 teams are engraved onto each band. When a band is full, the oldest band is removed and new one is added to the bottom. The first winning team on each band is displayed theoretically for 65 years.

43

Across

1. A D.C. NHL player (short)
5. Hockey HOF ind. 1993, (C) Edgar Lap___
9. Wild uniform red color name is Iron "R"
14. Hockey HOF ind. 1963, (C) Joe Pri___
15. Bruins Bill Gu___, 2001 NHL All-Star MVP
16. NHL Canucks C #40 "E" Pettersson
17. Pacific Coast Hockey League
18. A type of gambling, for e.g. office
19. NHL Predators D #57 Fabbro
20. Neatly holds cash for tix
22. Hockey - middle of the ice player (US sp)
23. Ducks vs Kings, known as the "F" Faceoff
25. Team merch $ may do this for low ticket sales
29. MTL missed the playoffs 1943-67
34. (Fr.) Long-time Avs D, Adam Foote NN
35. WCHL = ___n's Central Hockey League
37. Hockey HOF ind. 1990, (D) Fernie Fl___
38. "Check" in the offensive zone to gain puck
39. Fr Canes LW Battaglia's NN
40. 1924, the all Canadian NHL chose to ex___ to Boston
41. Hockey HOF ind. 1963, (D) Jack Laviol___
42. Rangers Mike G___er, 1993 NHL All-Star MVP
43. Stars alt Cpt Tyler Seguin NN
44. "Bruin", from "R" the Fox tale, means Brown
46. NHL on YT
47. Caps RW T.J. Oshie NN
50. NHL Golden Knights RW #19 "R" Smith
54. NHL Ducks C #14 Adam "H"
59. Spins w puck control, spin ___
60. Flame Milan Lucic NN - "M" Milan
61. Sens G Matt Murray NN
62. Hockey puck "became" on Feb 7th, 1876
63. Coyotes share Arizona w the NFL C___nals
64. "Burner" game, lots of goals scored
65. Score difference is only 1 goal
66. Measured Vitamin S, HGH
67. Detroit Red Wings are near this Great Lake

Down

1. Western Conference was the C___ell, pre 1993
2. NHL Oilers D #5 Cody
3. All American Hockey League
4. Do to goalie for extra attacker
5. Details about the game, e.g. sports page
6. "A part" in a hockey movie
7. Skills targets = LED - Light Emitting ___
8. 90's great - Erik Nicklas Lidström
9. Flight for a busy or late travel team
10. Ducks Teemu S___ne, 1998 NHL All-Star MVP
11. 80s ___endo console w Blades of Steel VG
12. Hockey HOF ind. 1978, (RW) Andy Bath___
13. Canucks Brock Bo___, 2018 NHL All-Star MVP
21. Hockey HOF ind. 2004, (D) Paul Co___
22. Hurricanes NN
24. 12 have their names on Stanley Cup
25. "Get your tickets here, $50"
26. (Fr.) Long-time Avs D, Adam "F" AKA Footer
27. 40-___ club, for goals and assists
28. Ret. Blue, Leaf Alexander "S" AKA Fixer
30. How old games were recorded
31. Prominent on hockey card
32. Devils Andreas Johnsson NN
33. Columbus' 1997 naming contest funded by W___, fast-food restaurant
35. Ret. RW Joel Ward NN
36. NHL Ottawa Senators on the scoreboard
39. Hockey HOF ind. 1965, (C) Marty B
43. Hockey HOF ind. 2007, (C) Mark Mes___
45. A Baltimore WHA player, 1975
46. NHL Sabres C #29 Hinostroza
48. 1974 Adams Award Winner, PHI
49. Game info on TV screen - "H" Up Display
50. Avalanche share Colorado w NFL B___os
51. Ottawa Senators logo is a Roman Gen___
52. Coyotes share Arizona w MLB D___ndbacks
53. Hockey HOF ind. 1972, (G) Hap Ho___
55. Wild share Minn. with the NBA T___rwolves
56. Off. defense that plays the point, a ___terback
57. Hockey HOF ind. 2001, (RW) Jari K___
58. NHL Red Wings LW #73 Adam "E"
60. Ret. Fr Pens C Maxime Talbot NN "M" Max

PUZZLE 21

1	2	3	4		5	6	7	8		9	10	11	12	13
14					15					16				
17					18					19				
20				21					22					
				23				24						
25	26	27	28					29			30	31	32	33
34					35	36				37				
38					39					40				
41					42				43					
44				45					46					
				47			48	49						
50	51	52	53			54				55	56	57	58	
59					60					61				
62					63					64				
65					66					67				

Hockey Fact: Each NHL team has a salary cap limit of $81.5 USD and can dress 23 players. Each team can have up to 50 players on a contract including NHL and minor league affiliates.

45

Across

1. Sony PlayStation Hockey VG "D"
5. TV cameras have them, power "line"
9. CAN won a gold one at 2002 Olympics
14. Red Wings share DET w the NBA P___ns
15. Kings share L.A. w the NBA L___s
16. Arena concession's is air-born
17. Song in US arenas, Star ___gled Banner
18. Hockey HOF ind. 1966, (C) Ted Ken___
19. 17yr Fr C Scott "G" AKA Gomer
20. NHL Blues' Training facility, ___ Community Ice Center
22. HOF ind. 1959, (LW) Cy "D" (CAN)
24. HOF G Ken Dryden received ___ Canada honors 2020
25. 90's was the "time" of increasing salaries
26. "Spot" of the arena, locale
27. Hat trick type, all in one period
32. HOF ind. 2012, (C) Adam "O" (CAN)
34. "Serious" injury AKA
35. NHL Avalanche GM, "J" Sakic
36. "T" Green, left NHL for WHA in yr 1
37. NHL Lightning D #81 Erik "C"
41. Ottawa fans red rallies, at City Hall "P"
44. Capitals owner - Chairman Ted "L"
46. Hockey HOF ind. 2015, (D) Nicklas Lids___ (Swe)
47. 90's great - Erik Nicklas Lidström
48. A contract do-over
52. Equipment place when the game is over
56. Kings mascot #72 is for LA's "A" temperature
57. Hurricanes NN
58. Fr host "D" Hodge, of TSN's That's Hockey
60. Sec. 233 Devils fans wear Triple D___ jerseys
61. CGY Saddledome went through one in 1994
62. G "Glen" Hall's misspelling on Stanley Cup
63. CHL = ___inental Hockey League
64. NHL Devils D #55 Geertsen
65. Bruins NN "Beasts of the ___"
66. Stars share Dallas w the MLB R___rs

Down

1. Fr. player & Head Coach "D" Dan Bylsma
2. NHL - WHA merger had a D___sal draft
3. Do for the anthem
4. NHL playoffs, a bracketed what?
5. Vancouver Canucks derogatory NN
6. Fr. QC Nordiques, brewer owner Carling "O"
7. USA flag in arena, the ___ white & blue
8. HOF ind. 1983, (G) Ken "D" (CAN)
9. Bruins 1st owner Adams, a grocery "M"
10. M. Berg___, QC Nordiques coach 1980-87
11. Calgary's Scotiabank Saddle what?
12. Pre game team prayer, ending
13. Why pro players get fat in the off-season
21. Great Lake Detriot Red Wings are near
23. Modern and pre-modern pro hockey "E"
28. BB cards are not ___ light resistant
29. Pro hockey legend Wayne G___ky
30. NHL maps each franchise their own "A"
31. Skills targets since 2019 - "Light Emitting Diode"
32. Oliver Oscar Emanuel Ekman-Larsson
33. Houston WHA player, 1972-78
35. 90's great - John Clark LeClair
38. "NickName" e.g. of team, players: Abbr
39. "A year" of play in the NHL AKA
40. 1996 Clancy Trophy Winner, WPG
41. Game pucks are frozen to ___ bounce
42. Hockey HOF ind. 1950, (C) Joe Ma___
43. 2002 Olympics location, CAN wins gold
45. No skate hockey, sitting in a chassis
46. NHL Coyotes C #72 Boyd
49. Coyotes NN Biz's Wagon
50. HGH, is for anti what?
51. Capitals Head Coach Peter Lavio___
52. A lot of NHL memorabilia, unfortunately is a?
53. Blues alt Cpt Vladimir Tarasenko NN
54. Cincinnati cycl___, Sabres ECHL affl.
55. CGY Saddledome went through one in 1994
59. 90's great - "Anthony Lewis Amonte"

PUZZLE 22

Hockey Fact: The NHL has 31 teams, 630 players on its Game Roster, & 713 players on its Active Roster. Of the 23 Active Roster players, only 20 (18 skaters + 2 goalies) are allowed to suit up for each team per game.

Across

1. Bruins David P___nak, 2020 All-Star MVP

5. Fake tickets

10. NHL Stars D #4 "M" Heiskanen

14. Sabres Daniel Br___, 2007 All-Star MVP

15. Don Rickles was, and said "Don't be a Hockey Puck" in 1995's Toy Story

16. NHL HOF Yzerman, born in ___brook BC

17. NYC WHA player, 1972-73

19. Jagr owns HC Klando of this league: Abbr

20. Midway - ar___ NHL Blitz game

21. WHA franchises, notoriously "un" what?

22. Play-by-play guy does from what he sees

24. Periods, eras or "A" in hockey

26. Stanley Cup originally for "Domi___ Hockey Challenge Cup"

27. A San Diego WHA Player, 1974-77

31. NHL Panthers goal-song

35. NHL Devils D #28 "D" Severson

36. Fr Pen & Wild Pascal Dupuis NN

38. KY Derby winning horse Go For "G" ate from Lord Stanley's Cup, 1994

39. Lightning used to share TB w the MLS M___y

40. Edmonton NHL player

41. Stanley Cup visited Russert's "___ the Press"

42. Groin injury is actually this body part

43. Gordie Howe passed his Hockey ones onto Mark Howe

44. NHL Senators C #12 Shane "P"

45. Personnel exchanges

47. Penguins AHL Affl Penguins in "S" PA

49. Apply a number to a player's skill

51. NHL Predators RW #28 "E" Tolvanen

52. QC Nordiques vs Canadiens 1984 "___ Saint" famous brawl

56. Team cheerleader in a costume

60. Gordie Howe, lesser known NN, "P___"

61. 90's great - "Raymond Garfield Sheppard"

62. NHL Senators city

63. EA Sports NHL VG Sony gaming platform

64. The worst teams are often the ___ popular

66. 0-0 score

67. Bruins Head Coach, Bruce C___dy

68. 2003 Jennings Trophy Winner, PHI

69. Hockey HOF ind. 1984, (G) Bernie Pa___

Down

1. Game "appears" on TV

2. Fan butt goes in one

3. NHL Wild's Training facility, ___ Rink

4. Fr. Hab & 33yr MI Coach Red Brenson NN

5. TV "window" AKA

6. NHL Colorado Avalanche State: Abbr

7. Team's pre game prayer, ending

8. Flame Milan Lucic AKA Mean "M"

9. Hockey HOF ind. 1962, (LW) Sweeney "S"

10. NHL Kraken LW #16 Jared "M"

11. Penguins share Pittsburgh w the MLB P___es

12. Hockey HOF ind. 1993, (C) Edgar Lap___

13. Cincinnati cycl___, Sabres ECHL affl.

18. Street for the 'Red Mile' Ottawa Senators fans

23. Lion-like noise from fan after a goal

25. 2018 Clancy Trophy Winner, VAN

27. Tix info, age descriptor related to price

28. Alma ___, college hockey

29. 1988 'Wayne Gretzky Hockey' VG, on "A"

30. Steroid use is against them

32. Represents a player

33. NHL Sharks LW #83 Matt "N"

34. NHL Senators G #31 "A" Forsberg

37. NHL Hurricanes D #22 Brett "P"

40. NHL Red Wings D #82 Jordan "O"

41. HOF G Ken Dryden, '04 Liberal Cabinet "M"

43. Team equipment AKA

44. NHL Lightning LW #18 Ondrej "P"

46. Oiler alt. Cpt Leon Draisaitl NN

48. Viewer tool, flips to other games

50. All 4 are checked by hockey card grader

52. Blues alt Cpt Vladimir Tarasenko NN

53. Hockey HOF ind. 1989, (LW) Herbie L___

54. Goalies protect them

55. NHL Ducks C #21 "I" Lundestrom

57. Sports fans basement get-away, a man___

58. "O" Nolan, drafted 1990 by QC Nordiques

59. EA Sports hit VG '94 Mu___ League Hockey

65. Short handed, stat

PUZZLE 23

1	2	3	4		5	6	7	8	9		10	11	12	13
14					15						16			
17				18			19				20			
21							22			23				
			24			25		26						
27	28	29					30		31			32	33	34
35						36		37				38		
39					40						41			
42				43						44				
45			46				47		48					
			49			50		51						
52	53	54				55			56			57	58	59
60					61				62					
63					64			65			66			
67					68						69			

Hockey Fact: The first Stanley Cup awarded to an NHL champion was in 1926. Before then it was awarded to the top amateur clubs, and NHA vs PCHA as far back as 1893

Across

1. 1974 Bill Masterson Trophy, MTL's Rocket
7. Offer pro incentive to stay w team
12. Concession burger w "oink-oink"
13. Hockey HOF ind. 2007, (C) Mark Mes___
14. VAN '90 1st rd pick, 18th overall, Shawn "A"
17. ___lade's 'Brett Hull Hockey' VG 1993
18. NHL online ___ com
19. Upper body injury area
21. Flames J. Gaudreau AKA "H" & Cheese
22. NHL Blackhawks goal-song, Chelsea "D"
26. NHL Red Wings RW #48 "G" Smith
28. Earned by players, given by league
29. Hockey appeals to young & old fans ___
30. Preds share Nashville with the NFL ___ns
31. A contract do-over
34. Trade rumors, often ___ymous
35. 90's great - "Michael Thomas Richter"
36. Capitals AHL affl Her___ Bears
38. LAK 1985 1st rd pick, 10th overall, Dan "G"
41. They get your second ticket
42. Jaws ___ is heard during Sharks PP
43. NHL Avalanche LW #75 Sampo "R"
44. NHL Canucks RW #6 Brock "B"
45. "Composite" of new/proposed arena
46. 80's great - "Alf Tomas Jonsson"
48. 80's great - "Mats Torsten Näslund"
49. (Ret.) Shane Albert Doan
50. O___us are thrown onto ice at Wings games
52. Ret. VAN G Kirk McLean play style
55. Helmets try to prevent it
56. 1980 NHL All-Star MVP, Flyers Reggie "L"
57. Injury in Joe Sakic's rookie year 1988-89
58. NHL on YouTube

Down

2. NHLPA's big contract: Abbr
3. Killing a penalty AKA short what?
4. Hollywood option for ceremonial puck drop
5. Fan support for team. Also, tree part
6. Did Not Start (game)
8. NHL Stars D #23 "E" Lindell
9. US state of ___gan has 2 teams in the OHL
10. 1997 Selke Trophy Winner, BUF, Mike "P"
11. HOF ind. 2015, (D) Nicklas Lids___ (Swe)
15. NHL Oilers RW #56 "K" Yamamoto
16. HOF ind. 1958, (C) Dick "I" (CAN)
20. Maple Leafs NN, "M" Beliefs
22. Stats AKA
23. A Detroit NHL player (short)
24. Ret. fr Oiler Cpt Jason Smith NN
25. NHL Sabres Head Coach Don "G"
26. HOF ind. 2001, (RW) Mike "G" (CAN)
27. Sports reporter AKA
32. Fits inside a hockey glove
33. Capitals Head Coach Peter Lavio___
35. Historic "point" or brief time in game
37. Each NHL "season"
39. Opponents
40. NHL "checks" for PEDs
43. Wear on trading card will "R" its value
44. Sabres LW Anders "B" AKA Bjorkie
45. Fr Red Wing Al Arbour NN, wore glasses on ice
46. American Collegiate Hockey Association
47. Hockey HOF ind. 1963, (D) Jack Ru___
49. Sport___, Canadian broadcaster of NHL
51. 90's great - "Patrick Michael LaFontaine"
53. (Ret.) Alexander Lennart Steen"
54. Pacific Hockey Association

PUZZLE 24

Hockey Fact: Hockey may be ruled by Canadian players but not its franchises! The Montreal Canadian were the last Canadian team to win the Stanley Cup back in 1993.

Across

1. Penguins state (short)
5. Concession soda tools
11. Flame Milan Lucic AKA Mean "M"
12. Ret. Flyer, TV analyst Chris "T" AKA Bundy
14. AB native, 2020 HOF inductee Iginla
15. Accepted reason to opt-out of All-Star game
16. A Indianapolis WHA player, 1974-78
17. 1970s Flyers NN, Broad St___ Bullies
18. Rangers in the NHL, Knicks in the what?
19. HOF Aubrey Victor Clapper NN
20. NHL Sabres RW #72 "T" Thompson
21. NHL Blue Jackets D #22 Jake "B"
22. Sens used to share Ottawa w CFL R___ades
24. Rangers share "New York" w the NFL Gi___
25. Hockey HOF ind. 1969, (G) Roy Wor___
26. Bruins alt Cpt Brad Marchand AKA "N" Face Killah
27. Winnipeg NHL player
28. Coach vs coach strategy match (slang)
29. Hockey HOF ind. 1990, (LW) Bill Ba___
31. Blackhawks name, from this Native Nation
32. Concession rule, usually 2-beer
34. Fan reaction to NYI 1995-97 fisherman logo
35. HOF ind. 1971, (LW) Gordon Rob___
39. Ducks Teemu S___ne, 1998 All-Star MVP
40. Calgary's Scotiabank Saddle what?
41. 33rd pick 2005, James "___ Deal" Neal
42. Trade rumors, often ___ymous
43. Celebrating team will dog___ the hero
44. 90's great - "Anthony Lewis Amonte"
45. 80's great - "Richard (Rick) Claude Vaive"
46. NHL Avalanche C #17 Tyson
47. NHL Stars G #70 "B" Holtby
50. Penguins NN
52. ___ Salaries, why Nordiques moved to Denver
53. 2006 Bill Masterson Trophy Winner, ANA
54. Represents player
55. Flyers 1981-83 Cooperall pants, banned for?
56. Concession till noise

Down

1. Penguins share Pittsburgh w MLB what?
2. Nordiques chose to r___ate to Denver 1995
3. ID on jersey
4. Song in US arenas, Star Spangled Ba___
5. Ret. Hawk Kris Versteeg NN
6. Don Cherry, 3_ years on Coach's Corner
7. Players do this on the bench between shifts
8. 90's great - "Adam Robert Oates"
9. Rewarded the Stanley Cup after playoffs
10. Canes C Sebastian Aho's NN
11. NHL Penguins D #6 John "M"
13. Hockey HOF ind. 1965, (F) Fred Sca___
14. NHL Kraken C #17 "J" Schwartz
15. HOF ind. 1966, (D) Babe "P" (CAN)
20. Hockey HOF ind. 2001, (RW) Mike Gar___
21. Fr. Ranger Pat Verbeek's NN
23. Oiler alt. Cpt Leon Draisaitl heritage
24. A hockey player in Winnipeg
25. Mid week game night (short)
28. Midway - ar___ NHL Blitz game
30. Arena waste holder
31. Leafs and Marlies (AHL) city
32. Avalanche NN
33. NHL Kings goal-song
34. Kings share L.A. w the NFL what? NN
36. Flyers ECHL affl Royals in "R" PA
37. Players (of a team) AKA
38. Term "Canuck" means Canadian, this way
40. Ducks franchise founder
42. E"A" Sports NHL video game publisher
43. NHL Lightning C #21 Brayden "P"
46. Meeting month for Hockey HOF induction committee
47. NHL Flames RW #15 "B" Richardson
48. 1942-67 NHL, O___nal Six (teams)
49. A Ottawa NHL player (short)
51. Hawks G Marc A Fleury NN

PUZZLE 25

Hockey Fact: Competing with the NHL for talent, the (PCHA) Pacific Coast Hockey Association existed in Western Canada and US between 1911 – 1924, before merging with the (WCHL) Western Canada Hockey League.

Across

1. Play-by-play guy is one
7. Sabres LW Jeff Skinner NN
11. Expansion team entry payment
12. Fr. Duck, Jet Finnish Flash, T___ Selanne
13. Brendan S___han, 1994 All-Star Skills Shot Accuracy winner
14. Bruins NN "Beasts ___" (3wd)
17. Joe Sakic, ___edited role in Sandler's Happy Gilmore
18. Hockey HOF ind. 1975, (D) Pierre Pi___
19. NYI 1995-97 fisherman logo resembled a "F" stick company
20. NHL Ducks RW #19 Troy "T"
22. NHL Kings D #8 "D" Doughty
23. Statement "Players do not take PEDs"
24. Do/done w the sports page
25. Ticket number-bar
28. A D.C. NHL player (short)
31. KY Derby winning horse Go For Gin, ___ from the Stanley Cup, 1994
32. QC Nordiques Rocket Richard games coached
33. # of ARZ Coyotes Stanley Cups (Spanish)
34. 64 Leafs Kelly, infant ___ peed in Stanley Cup
35. Paints hockey portraits
38. Ret. 8-team G Ron Tugnutt NN
40. Concession beer enforced rule
41. 15yr fr. Sen, Chris "N" AKA Neiler
43. 80's great - "Larry Clark Robinson"
44. AHL Belleville Senators on the scoreboard
45. NHL-NHLPA Collective Bargaining A___ment
46. Fr. G Felix Potvin's NN
50. NHL pre WHA had M___oly on hockey talent
52. 1988 'Wayne Gretzky Hockey' VG, system
54. Hockey HOF ind. 1959, (LW) Cy Den___
55. Announcer/anchor "retell" of the game AKA
57. Stanley Cup tickets can be ___ $5k
59. Tix info, related to tax (short)
60. Rodents found in old arenas

61. ESPN/TSN show at 2:30PM daily, "___ Interruption"
63. Capitals share D.C. w MLB N___nals
64. Hockey HOF ind. 1963, (RW) Jack Dar___
65. Blues Cpt Ryan O'Reilly NN
66. NHL Oilers C #29 "L" Draisaitl
67. Long time last place, cellar ___ (rhyme)

Down

1. Exhibition games happen vs Season
2. The "B" on a Bruins jersey
3. 1975-79 WHA Cincinnati Stingers logo
4. Concession burger type
5. Contact through NHL.com
6. Fr. Canuck Pavel "___ Rocket" Bure
7. G Brodeur has 125 career ___outs
8. Hawks alt Cpt. Patrick Kane AKA
9. Player salaries will "I" yearly due to inflation
10. Play-by-play guy's role, of what he sees
11. A broke team, likely result
15. 40 yr play-by-play, Hockey Night in Canada
16. Pepsi Center NN, Denver (Avs)
21. Hockey HOF ind. 1983, (G) Ken Dr___
26. A Detroit NHL player (short)
27. Non winner
29. Tix info, age descriptor
30. How flag is shown on NHL jersey
35. Ottawa Senators logo, from Roman Empire
36. New city for team to play in, move
37. Same score after 3 periods
39. NHL Predators C #13 Yakov "T"
40. NYR Marian G___ik, 2012 All-Star MVP
42. Kings 1990s mascot Kingston, a Snow what?
47. Montreal Canadiens Bell "C", cap 21K
48. Sits at SportsCenter desk
49. NHL Canadiens RW #73 "T" Toffoli
51. Knights LW Max Pacioretty AKA "P" Ready
53. Concession soda tool
56. HOF ind. 1963, (D) Bullet Joe Sim___
58. Kings share L.A. w the MLB D___rs
62. Ontario Hockey League

PUZZLE 26

Hockey Fact: Since 1914–15, the Stanley Cup has been won a total of 104 times by 20 existing NHL teams & five former existing teams.

Across

1. Player falls AKA to blow a what?
5. Like a 'slap'-shot, but w no windup
9. NHL Sharks C #48 "T" Hertl
14. Try-outs are a player ___ situation (short)
15. 1990s NHL Breakaway VG series by ___ aim
16. A ID on the back of a hockey jersey
17. Sharks entrance song by these "Metal" men
19. Ret. 14yr George Laraque NN
20. These friendly games don't count
21. Represents a player
22. AHL Toronto Marlies on the scoreboard
23. EHL = ___ Hockey League
25. Draft pick will soon be, to new team
29. Ticket object-locale info
33. Avalanche share Colorado w NFL B___ os
34. NHL Predators RW #28 "E" Tolvanen
36. Do to Lacrosse balls to make pucks, 1800s
37. NHL Anaheim Ducks on the scoreboard
38. NHL Islanders D #24 "S" Mayfield
40. AHL Milwaukee Admirals on scoreboard
41. CBC's Battle of the Blades, Figure Skaters w Hockey players, event
44. Keith T___uk, '98 All-Star Shot Accuracy
45. Hockey HOF ind. 1945, (C) Howie Mo___
46. HOF 5ft 5in G Roy Worters fishy NN
48. Flyers Wells Fargo Arena NN
50. A player's pre-game warm-up ride (short)
52. Fan reaction to NYI '95-97 fisherman logo
53. EA Sports NHL game, programmer AKA
56. Scoreboard info display
62. NHL Flyers Head Coach "A" Vigneault
63. Sega console, played NHL 2K 2000 VG
64. ___ soft Xbox console w Hockey VG
65. HOF ind. 1971, (LW) Gordon Rob___
66. Flyers share Philadelphia w NFL E___ s
67. Caps RW T.J. Oshie NN
68. Athletes abandon theirs in the off-season
69. Hockey HOF ind. 1988, (RW) Guy LeF___

Down

1. Arena ice is set at -9 Celsius (short)
2. Hockey HOF ind. 1967, (RW) Harry Ol___
3. Apply a number to a player's skill
4. Band that holds jocks on
5. Rising what? = '95 Nordiques move to COL
6. Hockey HOF ind. 2007, (C) Ron Fra___
7. ___ lade made 'Brett Hull Hockey' VG 1993
8. Players travel city to city in it
9. NHL Maple Leafs C #91 John "T"
10. A narrow win amount
11. '95 Bruins unis = ho___ to Winnie the Pooh
12. Hockey HOF ind. 1990, (D) Fernie Fl___
13. Player complained, then was ___ off
18. NHL Oilers C #29 "L" Draisaitl
24. 2002 Olympics locale, CAN wins gold: Abbr
25. NHL Sharks LW #42 "J" Gadjovich
26. Station status when reporting game
27. Gold, may be hanging from player's what?
28. Possible player reaction after a win
30. Directly shoot a passed puck, a one- what?
31. Puck across 2 lines to Def. zone, no touch
32. Sens D Michael Del Zotto NN
33. Leafs share Toronto w the NBA what? NN
35. Retired players get it, want to scratch-return
39. Stars G Branden Holtby NN
42. 16yr 6-team Mike "R" AKA Mickey Ribs
43. ANA 2000 1st rd pick, 12th overall, Alexei
45. "Extreme" change needed for bad teams
47. "Penalty Kill", stat and unit type
49. Bruins LW Jake DeBrusk AKA Jake from State what?
51. Game has been "completed"
53. Blackhawks wear "C" jerseys on Veterans Day (short)
54. Penguin Greg P___, 1973 All-Star MVP
55. NHL Blackhawks C #77 Kirby "D"
57. Hockey HOF ind. 2001, (RW) Jari K___
58. NHL Senators D #98 Victor "M"
59. Slang for metal bars over helmet face
60. Markus N___nd won '02 All-Star Shot Acc.
61. Devils a___nate uniforms have green pants

PUZZLE 27

Hockey Fact: The Stanley Cup has more than 3000 different names, including over 1300 players engraved on it.

Across

1. Common bone / spinal hockey injury
5. Used to eat dessert at arena
10. Cap Cpt Alex Ovechkin NN "M" Bear
14. Hockey HOF ind. 1974, (LW) Dickie M___
15. A great goalie can "C" a weak team
16. Fan admiration action
17. No longer a team member, now a
19. NHL Islanders RW #15 "C" Clutterbuck
20. Enter arena through a "G"
21. Sec. 233 Devils fans wear "T" digit jerseys
22. A San Diego WHA Player, 1974-77
24. Fr. Canuck P___ Bure, the Russian Rocket
26. Trade rumors, often ___ ymous
27. Hockey HOF ind. 1962, (LW) Sweeney "S"
31. Fr. Canuck C Jannik Hansen, heritage
35. TSN "Hockey" program hosted by Gino Reda
36. Hockey HOF ind. 1950, (D) Graham Drink___
38. Roller Hockey Alliance
39. HOF ind. 1949, (D) Art "R" (CAN)
40. NYI 1995-97 logo resembled Cpt High___
41. Team branded "Stuff-We-All-Get"
42. "Also Known As" often for nicknames
43. Arena bins
44. Sarnia's OHL hockey team
45. NN Penncakes, fr. NHLer Dustin "P"
47. League's legal guy
49. Kraken city, S___ le
51. 1972 WHA Miami team, to P___delphia before ever playing a game
52. Dumping players decreases # of team's "S"
56. Phones into a sports radio show
60. Ottawa Senators logo, Roman Gen___
61. 90's great - "Stephen Antony Thomas"
62. Blainville-Boisbriand's QMJHL hockey team
63. HOF ind. 2003, (C) Pat LaFont___ (US)
64. NHL Bruins C #11 "T" Frederic
66. More players to rosters
67. Hockey HOF ind. 2001, (RW) Mike Gar___
68. Sports athletes & writers, awards
69. Hockey HOF ind. 2011, (C) Joe Nieuwe___

Down

1. Micro___ Xbox consoles, play Hockey VGs
2. Condition of low value hockey card
3. Hockey HOF ind. 2001, (RW) Jari K___
4. Quebec City's QMJHL hockey team
5. Stand in the goalies sight
6. NHL Pittsburgh Penguins State: Abbr
7. Canucks logo, AKA whale
8. Spins w puck control, spin ___
9. NHL Maple Leafs RW #88 William "N"
10. NHL Penguins LW #23 Brock "M"
11. Ducks Teemu S___ne, 1998 All-Star MVP
12. They get your second ticket
13. 1990s enforcer Stu Grimson AKA The Grim Re___
18. NHL Blue Jackets G #90 "E" Merzlikins
23. Lion-like noise from fans after a goal
25. LAK 2006 1st rd pick, 17th overall, Trevor "L"
27. Holds fighters jersey down
28. To lose when you shouldn't
29. HOF G Hasek NN
30. NHL Avalanche LW #75 Sampo "R"
32. NHL Capitals D #52 Matt "I"
33. NHL Senators C #12 "S" Pinto
34. Caps LW Carl Hagelin NN
37. Chiclets AKA
40. 1300 G, 18 Season A. Kovalev NN
41. NHL Coyotes D #86 Anton "S"
43. To ___ a mouth guard is not mandatory
44. Tampa Bay Lightning ECHL "S" Bears, Orlando
46. 33rd pick 2005, James Neal NN
48. Fr. NHL Hamilton Tigers NN
50. Emotional, wet fan reaction to big game loss
52. Fan butt goes in one
53. Kraken share Seattle w the MLB M___ers
54. NHL Sharks C #18 "L" Pederson
55. Arena climber
57. NHL Coyotes LW #16 Andrew "L"
58. Habs Joel Edmunson NN
59. NHL Wild C #49 Victor "R"
65. Gretzky's NHL city, 1996-99: Abbr

PUZZLE 28

1	2	3	4	█	5	6	7	8	9	█	10	11	12	13
14				█	15					█	16			
17				18		█	19				20			
21						█	22			23				
█	█	24			25		26				█	█		
27	28	29					30	█	31			32	33	34
35				█	36		37			█	38		
39				█	40					█	41		
42			█	43				█	44				
45			46			█	47		48				
█	█	49			50	█	51				█	█		
52	53	54				55	█	56			57	58	59
60				█	61		█	62					
63				█	64		65	█	66				
67				█	68			█	69				

Hockey Fact: 1973 WHA New Jersey Knights franchise's Cherry Hill Arena ice surface was slanted, rising up towards the center ice.

59

Across

1. Atlanta Gl___tors, Ottawa Sens ECHL affl
5. Fr. Flame Fleury's Battle of the Blades partner
9. Slapshots over 100 mph descriptor
13. Helmets to head shape
14. Stanley Cup uses Twitter to "send" info
16. Hockey HOF ind. 1985, (C) Jean Rat___
17. Don Cherry statements can be ___tical
18. Slapshot, the ___ mascot of Wash. Capitals
19. 33rd pick 2005, James "___ Deal" Neal
20. Same after 3 periods, needs a tie "B"
22. Al "I" 96 mph, won '96 All-Star Fastest Shot
24. Stanley Cup base is 5 stacked what?
26. 1932 Stanley Cup winner, Toronto Maple?
27. Summer hockey, non ice rink play
30. 10yr fr. ATL, WPG's Jim "S" AKA Slats
32. Pads must shock "A" to prevent injury
34. Avg of NHL'er is 28
35. HOF ind. 2008, (C) Igor Lari___ (Rus)
39. AHL Cleveland Monsters on the scoreboard
40. Gary Unger NN, played 914 consecutive gms
43. 90's great - "Adam Robert Oates"
44. Hockey HOF ind. 1969, (G) Roy Wor___
46. Attempts (short)
47. Maple Leafs NN
49. 1986 'Great Ice Hockey' on Sega "M" System
52. Pro hockey participants gender
53. Spectacular plays AKA
55. Schedules are full of them
57. Squared view of game seen from here
59. TV's WKRP in Cincinnati character "Les" has WHA Stingers sticker
63. HOF ind. 1961, (G) George Hainsw___
64. CGY Saddledome had major ones in 1994
66. Houston WHA player, 1972-78
67. QC Nordiques vs Canadiens in famous 1984 "Good Friday Mass___"
68. Hockey Night in Canada, 1952
69. "Happy"-ful fans. Also, TV show w dancing
70. Hockey HOF ind. 1985, (LW) Bert Olms___
71. Capitals share D.C. w MLB what? NN
72. Sharks entrance song is by M___lica

Down

1. Western Conference was C___ell pre 1993
2. Fans enter through it
3. HOF ind. 2009, (LW) Luc Robita___
4. A Devils fan in famed section 122
5. Ret. Blue & Leaf Alexander "S" AKA Fixer
6. Given to best players of the season
7. Groin injury is actually this body part
8. NHL Predators RW #28 "E" Tolvanen
9. NHL Sharks D #38 Mario "F"
10. A pro hockey player in Toronto
11. Glen Sather's playing days NN
12. "Vision" to watch game
15. Sharks "T.T." NN
21. NHL Avalanche C #91 Nazem "K"
23. Expansion team entry payment
25. 1973 WHA NJ Knight's odd ice surface
27. NHL "stat" AKA
28. The Hockey News AKA The B___
29. Canucks Brock Bo___, 2018 All-Star MVP
31. 90's great "Alexander Gennadevich Mogilny"
33. NHL Flyers C #19 Derick "B"
36. Mc___, brought Gretzky to the Kings, 1988
37. 1st black player in NHL, 1958
38. 1933 Calder Trophy Winner, DET
41. NHL Ottawa Senators on the scoreboard
42. IDs on the back of many jerseys
45. Puck "damaged" the glass on the boards
48. "The Hockey Sweater" content on C$5 bill
50. KY Derby, Belmont Stake winning horse Go For Gin, ___ from Stanley Cup in '94
51. Reason there's no tickets left to buy
53. "Jets" is for WPG's ties to the Air "F"
54. Pull the goalie for "one more" attacker
56. NHL "checks" for PEDs
57. Hawks, 1st to sound horn after G, horn type?
58. HOF has six___ On-Ice Officials, as of 2020
60. ___ed cheese on your concession nachos
61. NHL maps each franchise their own "A"
62. NHL Panthers C #55 "N" Acciari
65. Rangers in the NHL, Knicks in the?

PUZZLE 29

Hockey Fact: In 1892 the Governor General of Canada, Lord Stanley of Preston, donated the Dominion Hockey Challenge Cup and awarded it to the top amateur hockey club in Canada, the Montreal Hockey Club in 1893

Across

1. Trade rumors, often ___ ymous
5. Bobby Hull's 10yr $2.75M WHA contract
9. Blues alt Cpt Vladimir Tarasenko NN
13. Stanley Cup's champagne fruity ingredient
14. Stanley Cup awarded ___ season's playoffs
15. Bruins Head Coach, Bruce C___dy
16. Dallas Stars American Air___ Center
17. Devils, part of the M___politan Division
18. "Top" team, or top player AKA
19. NHL Canadiens C #71 Jake "E"
20. Emotional wet fan reaction to big game loss
22. Fr. Canuck C Jannik Hansen from "Denmark"
23. Roster has an injured & active one
24. 1977 movie 'Slap Shot', final scene exposure AKA Strip what?
27. NHL Blue Jackets Head Coach Brad "L"
29. NHL Coyotes RW #9 "C" Keller
31. Final score is zero (slang). Also, puck NN
32. HOF ind. 1977, (D) Tim "H" (CAN)
33. Flames haven't won the Stanley Cup ___ '89
36. HOF G Ken Dryden AKA the 4-"S" Goalie
37. Red Wings share DET w the NBA what?
39. Good seats means you ___ all the action
40. HOF ind. 1950, (D) Newsy "L" (CAN)
41. Police do with unruly fan at the game
45. Fits inside a hockey glove
46. Cleveland ___ters, Blue Jackets AHL affl.
48. "Burner" game, lots of goals scored
50. Shot hits top "area" of net
52. Said as upper or lower, in arena
53. Coyotes AHL affl Tucson R___unners
56. 80s Nint___ console had Blades of Steel VG
57. NHL Red Wings LW #15 Jakub "V"
58. 2x Cup winner w Pens, Caps - Brooks Orpik AKA "F" Candy
59. Kings share L.A. w the NBA L___s
60. Street for 'Red Mile' - Ottawa Senators fans
61. "Put together" a hockey team AKA

62. Stanley (Cup) of Preston, Royal designation
63. Already "watched" the game

Down

1. Oilers is one to the Flames, esp. 1980s
2. NHL Panthers goal-song (3wd)
3. First game of season
4. Senators 1st ever coach, Rick Bow___
5. One team vs another
6. Hockey HOF ind. 2012, (C) Adam "O"
7. Player removed from game roster
8. Ret. enforcer Chris Thorburn NN
9. Run it at the bar watching the game
10. A Ottawa NHL player
11. 90's great - "Ronald Scott Stevens"
12. BOS 1996 1st rd pick, 8th overall, Johnathan
13. Song for US teams, Star Span___ Banner
21. Flyers G Carter Hart AKA "S" Hart
23. Well-known veteran, retired player AKA
25. Detroit's NN, Hock___wn
26. PlayStation console w Hockey videogames
28. Ret. Leafs Cpt Phaneuf NN = Sloppy "S"
30. Non winners
33. Mark Messier NN, The Mes___
34. Elmont - Long Island, NY NHL player
35. Future HOF Joe 'Jumbo' Thor___
37. 2 teams vs, for the Stanley Cup
38. Fr. Gretzky protector, Dave "S"
39. NHL Senators LW #13 Zach "S"
42. NHL Kraken RW #7 Jordan "S"
43. WSH 1988 1st rd pick, 15th overall, Reggie
44. NHL Predators C #13 Yakov "T"
47. Father-time catches this player type
49. Hockey HOF ind. 1965, (F) Fred Sca___
51. Sit out when injured to do what?
52. Chicago Wo___, Hurricanes AHL affl team
54. 90's great - "Adam Robert Oates"
55. NHL Wild C #16 "R" Pitlick

PUZZLE 30

Hockey Fact: 1973 WHA New Jersey Knights Cherry Hill Arena had no Visiting Team dressing room. Opposition teams had to dress in a nearby hotel. Oh, and the arena glass was actually chicken wire.

Across

1. Calgary Saddledome (Flames) renamed to ___dian Airlines 1994

5. Joe Sakic, acted in Sandler's "Happy G___re"

9. Fr Canes LW Battaglia's NN

14. Tomas K___le, 2008 All-Star Skills Shot Accuracy winner

15. Sport bar's bright sign

16. On the back of a hockey jersey

17. A roll AKA ___ of 50-50 tickets

18. Team's win was written in the cards

19. Can't get it out of a jersey i.e. blood

20. NHL on TV

22. 7th pick 2005, Retired player Jack Skille NN

23. Score 3 & fans will throw hats where?

25. NHL Senators D #72 Thomas

29. Predators fans throw this seafood onto ice

34. HOF ind. 2014, (G) Dominik H (Czech)

35. Holds up - supports arena roof

37. Coyotes were nearly named Sc___ons

38. Carl H___in, 2012 All-Star Skills Fastest Skater

39. US state has a team in the OHL (short)

40. Hot indoor arena (slang)

41. 33rd pick 2005, James "___ Deal" Neal

42. Norfolk Admi___, Hurricanes ECHL affl team

43. "Time" in the NHL

44. Gordie Howe, most played NHL games w 23

46. Pens LW Jake Guentzel NN

47. Subs - #3 will play ___ of #33

50. Bruins 3rd jersey letter "B" design

54. Stanley Cup, oldest among NA pro sports trophies

59. TV remote noise

60. HOF ind. 1949, (C) Dan B (CAN)

61. Fr. Canuck P___ Bure, the Russian Rocket

62. Fr. Canuck, Pen Matt "C" AKA POS

63. NYI 95-97 logo mocked as G___ns Fishsticks

64. Celebrating team will dog___ the hero

65. Hockey HOF puts a ___ in the Builder category

66. Islander Mike B___, 1982 NHL All-Star MVP,

67. Hockey HOF ind. 1985, (C) Jean R

Down

1. 1990s Hockey VGs came on ___ridges

2. WHA Cincinnati Stingers logo

3. NHL Jets D #4 Pionk

4. Canadiens Head Coach Dom Duch___

5. 64 Leafs Kelly, ___ son urinated in Stanley Cup

6. Worst teams are often the ___ popular

7. Canadiens attachment to Flander Fields poem

8. NHL Washington Capitals Capital "O" arena

9. Uncommon slang for the net

10. HGH (PED), for aging excuse

11. Hurricanes Eric S___, 2008 NHL All-Star MVP

12. NHL Blue Jackets C #52 Bemstrom

13. Senators NN

21. HOF ind. 1952, (RW) Bill C (CAN)

22. Fake tickets

24. Don Cherry, 7 seasons w Rochester Amer___

25. Zedano "C" 109 mph, 2012 All-Star Skills Fastest Shot

26. NHL Blackhawks LW #38 Brandon

27. A Oakland NHL player, 1967-76

28. Flyers nearly intro'd as the Liberty what? 1966

30. TBL 2019 1st round pick, 27th overall, Nolan

31. 1953 Stanley Cup Champion Coach, MTL

32. The team "S" a lot to get the Free Agent

33. NHL Stars LW #24 Roope

35. Tampa Bay's ECHL Solar "B", Orlando

36. 90's great - Erik Nicklas Lidström

39. Locker room hijinx

43. Hole-filled top of arena draft beer

45. TV, sports scroller

46. 1978 Selke Trophy Winner Bob "G", MTL

48. Emotional fan reaction to big game loss

49. Fans file out of arena through them

50. ___lade's 'Brett Hull Hockey' VG 1993

51. Lose a game or lead

52. Spartacat, the ___ mascot of Ottawa Senators

53. World H___y Association, 1971-79

55. Wraps a stick handle

56. Blue Jackets, name inspired by C___ War

57. Hockey HOF ind. 1958, (G) Alec Con___

58. "Happy" fans. Also, TV show w dancing

60. Angry fan audio

PUZZLE 31

Hockey Fact: Mark Messier was the last NHL player to have ever played for the competing WHA. He played 52 games for the Indianapolis Racers & Cincinnati Stingers in 1978-79....then played his last NHL game on April 3, 2004

Across

1. AZ Coyotes were nearly named Sc___ons

5. Ligue Nord-Americaine re Hockey

9. 1977 Calder Trophy Winner, ATL

14. Lion-like noise from fan after a goal

15. English Ice Hockey Association

16. 2018 Vezina Trophy Winner, Nashville

17. Red, only used on the QC Nordiques what?

18. Ottawa Senators fans dress up, as Roman Le___arry

19. All 4 are checked by hockey card grader

20. Goal in "unattended net" AKA

22. Ice cream from arena concession

24. Ret. 16yr John LeClair, AKA Johnny "V"

25. Used to watch a game (sl.)

26. NHL Islanders D #4 "A" Greene

27. Hockey HOF ind. 1959, (LW) Cy "D"

32. Hurricanes NN

34. Sharks G James Reimer NN

35. 90's great - "Christopher Robert Pronger"

36. 80's great - "Anders Thomas Steen"

37. Bruins NN "___ of the East"

41. Contracts AKA

44. CCHA = ___ Collegiate Hockey Association

46. NHL Hurricanes D #25 Ethan

47. 90's great - "Anthony Lewis Amonte"

48. Miami Arena NN, Panthers

52. Works the arena's concession

56. Gretzky, the Greatest Of what?

57. NHL Flyers Head Coach "A" Vigneault

58. NHL New York Rangers ___son Square Garden

60. TB Lightening Girls, dance "U" until 2019

61. NHL Predators D #57 "D" Fabbro

62. Fr. Gretzky protector, Dave "C___thead" Semenko

63. "Maple Leaf" was owner Smythe's WW1 ___ment

64. Game "completed"

65. Hockey HOF ind. 1975, (RW) George Armst___

66. Penguins share Pittsburgh w the MLB P___es

Down

1. NHL Capitals D #9 Dmitry "O"

2. NHL Stars LW #24 "R" Hintz

3. NYI C Jean-Gabriel Pageau NN

4. Gary Unger NN, 914 consecutive games played

5. Great players of old

6. Ret. Flyers, TB G Antero Niittymaki NN

7. NHL Islanders D #25 Sebastian "A"

8. L or R e.g. shooting

9. The game is on "right-now"

10. HOF Nicklas Lidstrom NN

11. Stanley Cup orig. for "Dominion Hockey Chall___ Cup"

12. Hockey HOF ind. 2001, (RW) Mike Gar___

13. Fas___ Skater, All-Star Skills Comp. event

21. Forward passes allowed pre 1927 NHL

23. Used to watch a game

28. All-Star game 1998-2002, World vs?: Abbr

29. Sharks entrance song by M___lica

30. Fr NHL G, Ron Tugnutt's NN

31. Contract agreement

32. Fr. Flame Fleury, aboriginal heritage

33. Sami K___en, 2000 All-Star Skills Fastest Skater

35. Network of "Battle of the Blades" NHL + Figure skaters

38. Season Tickets

39. Anthem, best when a "T" singer performs

40. Player hit so hard, loses equip. = yard what?

41. Contract negotiating. Also, passing out playing cards

42. Thrashers Dany H___ey, 2003 All-Star MVP

43. NHL Canadiens LW #62 "A" Lehkonen

45. Press consensus best NHL #28, Steve "L"

46. NHL Stars G #70 "B" Holtby

49. Hockey HOF ind. 1962, (LW) Sweeney Sch___

50. 1988 'Wayne Gretzky Hockey' VG, on "A"

51. VAN '82 1st rd pick, 11th overall, Michel "P"

52. Midway - ar___ NHL Blitz game

53. Ducks Teemu S___ne, 1998 NHL All-Star MVP

54. Derek ___erson, left NHL for WHA year 1

55. '87 Jets fans, dubbed "Winnipeg W___out"

59. Alexander Mikhailovich Ovechkin

PUZZLE 32

1	2	3	4		5	6	7	8		9	10	11	12	13
14					15					16				
17					18					19				
20				21				22	23					
24								25						
			26					27			28	29	30	31
	32	33							34					
35												36		
37			38	39	40			41	42	43				
44					45	46								
			47				48				49	50	51	
52	53	54	55				56							
57					58	59				60				
61					62					63				
64					65					66				

Hockey Fact: Like the multi-colored balls of the ABA - NBA's competing basketball league, the NHL's competitor WHA of 1972-79 experimented with blue-colored pucks. These were thought to be easier for fans to see. These pucks are highly sought after collectors items

Across

1. Markus N___nd, 2002 All-Star Skills Shot Accuracy winner
5. NHL Anaheim Ducks "H" Center, cap 17K
10. Amateur Hockey Association of Canada
14. TB Lightning Girls, dance "U" until 2019
15. NHL Coyotes D #86 "A" Stralman
16. NHL Rangers C #93 "M" Zibanejad
17. Pub AKA
19. Heads Up Display (on TV): Abbr
20. Common gambling term
21. CGY (Flames) Saddledome, 1983
22. Middle of the Bruins 8-spoke wheel (3wd)
24. Ticket at a discount, AKA on what?
26. Penguins share Pittsburgh w MLB P___es
27. Teammates may collide, purely by "A"
31. Hockey, Football, Baseball
35. Bruins tune "Time To Go" used for what?
36. Seen on the schedule
38. Players enter camp ___ of shape
39. Game on this early week night (short)
40. Concession no-beef burger
41. Joe Sakic, acted in Sandler's "Happy Gil___"
42. NHL Stars D #23 "E" Lindell
43. NHL Penguins D #4 Taylor "F"
44. TB Lightning Girls squad type, until 2019
45. NHL Devils C #18 Dawson "M"
47. NHL Sharks C #18 Lane "P"
49. Angry fan audio, snake-like
51. Hockey HOF ind. 2007, (D) Scott Ste___
52. Ret. Hab Mats Naslund AKA ___ Viking
56. A Los Angeles WHA player, 1972-74
60. 1st black player in NHL, 1958
61. Press consensus best NHL #4, Bobby "O"
62. Show before the game
63. Capitals share D.C. w the MLB what? NN
64. 11yr North Star Lou "N" AKA Sweet Lou
66. Point to point mark made on telestrator
67. "Happy" fans. Also, TV show w dancing
68. Slap Shot movie, Newman's language, a lot
69. 2002 Olympics "Salt" location, CAN won gold

Down

1. Red Wings wheel logo, tribute to "A" industry
2. Like a "slap"-shot, but w no windup
3. Seeing a hockey game in-person
4. Tools used to eat concession meals
5. Thin length of a stick
6. NHL Toronto Maple Leafs Province: Abbr
7. Hockey HOF ind. 1960, (D) Sylvio Ma___
8. Ret. 14yr George Laraque NN
9. NHL Hurricanes G #31 Frederik "A"
10. Canadiens attachment to Flander Fields poem
11. Arena on game day, a bee ___ of activity
12. Kings share L.A. w the NBA L___s
13. Player's energy source (sl, short)
18. Knights LW Max Pacioretty AKA Patio "R"
23. Concession beer servers
25. Game "completed"
27. NHL Senators D #2 "A" Zub
28. 50-50 tix often supports a local "C"
29. NHL Sabres goal-song, Let me ___ my throat
30. Return to the neutral zone, avoid offside
32. Fr. MTL Maroons NN
33. 2006 NHL Foundation Player Winner, DAL
34. Ret. Blue, Leaf Alexander "S" AKA Fixer
37. NHL Flames D #8 Christopher "T"
40. The Hockey News, print & online
41. HOF ind. 1965, (C) Jack "M" (CAN)
43. A lot of player memorabilia is counter___
44. Padding in a helmet
46. Concession nacho topper
48. Contract negotiator. Also, hands out cards
50. Concession soda tool
52. NA Ice Rinks, 200 ft "L" x 85ft wide
53. Ottawa Senators logo, Roman Gen___
54. Former mascot of the Pittsburgh Penguins
55. NHL Red Wings LW #73 Adam "E"
57. Atlanta Gl___tors, Ottawa Sens ECHL affl
58. The playing surface, or arena AKA
59. Common mid leg injury, MCL, ACL
65. All-Star game 1998-2002, World vs?: Abbr

PUZZLE 33

Hockey Fact: Glow Puck or Glowing Puck's official name was FoxTrax. This lit puck was part of FOX SPORTS telecast to make the puck more visible to casual fans. The concept was heavily criticized. Having started at the 1996 All-Star game it ended at the conclusion of the 1997-98 Playoffs.

Across

1. Place in NHL HQ, review game tapes
7. EDM 1986 1st rd pick, 21st overall, Kim "I"
12. NHL Bruins LW #56 Erik "H"
13. Houston WHA player, 1972-78
14. A Cherry Hill NJ WHA player, 1973-74
17. Krakens Brandon Tanev NN
18. (FA) Eric Craig Staal
19. "All Rights Reserved", NHL logo &branding
21. WHA Cincinnati Stingers logo
22. Goalies blocker AKA what? pad
26. Arena climb obstacles
28. "The Hockey Sweater" takes place in "R" QC
29. Mascot fires one from an air cannon
30. Hockey HOF ind. 2012, (C) Adam O___
31. Team's will "R" unneeded player(s)
34. Each one holds up the net's crossbar
35. NHL HQ located in "M" town Manhattan
36. 6-team fr. goalie Dwayne Roloson NN
38. NHL Kraken C #15 Riley "S"
41. Low scoring game is, to many fans
42. The team "S" a lot to get the Free Agent
43. Fr. Canuck C Jannik Hansen AKA "H" Badger
44. Toronto's team name before Maple Leafs, 1919-27 (short)
45. 1997 All-Star Skills Fastest Skater, Peter "B"
46. NHL San Jose Sharks ___ Center, cap 18K
48. 80's great - "Steven Donald Larmer"
49. AHL Milwaukee Admirals on the scoreboard
50. J Sakic, un___ited in Sandler's Happy Gilmore
52. Ret. Leafs Cpt Dion Phaneuf NN Sloppy "S"
55. Top coach type
56. Coach and Ref over bad call
57. Concession nachos nutritional units (short)
58. Kings 1990s mascot Kingston, a Snow "L"

Down

2. Roller Hockey Alliance
3. ANA 2011 1st rd pick, 30th overall Rickard "R"
4. 6 "O" pucks are NHL regulation weight
5. Penguin Greg P___, 1973 All-Star MVP
6. 90's great - "Michael Alfred Gartner"
8. Weekend game night (short)
9. 15yr fr. Hawk Brent Seabrook NN
10. NHL Red Wings LW #73 Adam "E"
11. Score less result
15. Fan feeling toward rival team
16. "Behind" in score
20. A Mascot fires a p___ from an air cannon
22. Concession bread food
23. Pro players operate fancy ones
24. Substitute player's energy. Also, edible fruit
25. All-Star Skills Comp. event, "F" Skater
26. Fast action drill(s) type
27. HOF ind. 1966, (D) Ken "R" (CAN)
32. Kraken, inspired by giant Puget "S" Octopus
33. NHL Capitals C #20 Lars "E"
35. Where to keep a trophy
37. NHL Maple Leafs RW #65 "I" Mikheyev
39. NHL mobile offerings, several (short)
40. Game info on TV screen - ___ Up Display
43. Fans do it with signs
44. Jab opponent with stick blade
45. Ret. 19yr Goalie, Roberto Luongo NN "B" Bango Bongo Luongo
46. Syracuse Crunch Hockey Club
47. NHL maps each franchise their own "A"
49. NYR 1987 1st rd pick, 10th overall Jayson "M"
51. (Ret.) Daniel Denis Boyle
53. NHL Lightning D #52 "C" Foote
54. Kraken uniform, Deep "S" Blue

PUZZLE 34

Hockey Fact: The fastest recorded slapshot is Bobby Hull's, registering 118 miles per hour in 1963. This is 10-15mph faster than most of the fastest recorded today so this record is up for great debate.

Across

1. Canadian Amateur Hockey Association

5. Steroid users get labeled as these

11. NYR owner - Chairman James "D"

12. AHL Bears PA location

14. HOF ind. 1961, (R) Frank "R" (CAN)

15. NHL Hurricanes D #77 Tony "D"

16. "All" 3 periods of a game

17. Scott N___rmayer, 1998 All-Star Skills Fastest Skater

18. The Hockey News editor

19. Mascots fire t-shirts from "A" cannons

20. Add to a team's negative column

21. Original Six era, the owners control was seen as a ___poly

22. Lightning alt. Cpt "Victor Erik Olof Hedman"

24. Backup goalie will w bench most games (slang)

25. Senators fans dress up, Roman Le___arry

26. NHL-NHLPA C___ctive Bargaining Agreement

27. Fr Capitals G Jim Carey NN

28. 2018 Vezina Trophy Winner, NSH

29. Hockey HOF ind. 2020, (RW) Jarome Ig___

31. Coyotes uniform accent color, name

32. Hurricanes NN

34. Performance Enhancing Drug

35. HOF ind. 1971, (LW) Gordon Rob___

39. Cincinnati cycl___, Sabres ECHL affl.

40. NYR alt. Cpt Mika Zibanejad NN

41. 1970s Flyers NN, Broad St___ Bullies

42. Hockey HOF ind. 1990, (D) Fernie Fl___

43. WHL = ___ern Hockey League

44. Admission price AKA

45. AHL Springfield Thunderbirds on scoreboard

46. Panthers share Miami w the NBA what?

47. NHL Flyers Captain "C" Giroux

50. Sens C Chris Tierney AKA (snake)

52. Fr. Canuck C Jannik "H" AKA Honey Badger

53. From QC Nordiques to Avalanche 1995

54. St. Louis Blues ___prise Center, cap 19K

55. Gretzky's WHA team, 1978-79

56. Concession does for arena patrons

Down

1. Room for broadcasting

2. Evgeni M___, 2009 All-Star Skills Shot Accuracy winner

3. Physical feature hidden under helmet

4. HOF ind. 2017, (RW) Teemu Sel___ (Fin)

5. Coyotes alt. Cpt Phil Kessel NN

6. Stars ECHL Affl. Idaho Steel___

7. NHL Red Wings LW #73 Adam "E"

8. 90's great - "Adam Scott Graves"

9. 4 Cup winner Chris Kunitz NN

10. 2006 Bill Masterson Trophy Winner, ANA

11. Canuck twin "D" Sedin

13. Fr 5-team G Johan Hedberg NN (string toy)

14. NYR Ryan Reaves NN

15. Skills targets = LED - Light Emitting ___

20. Napoleon rep___ cannon fired at Columbus Blue Jackets games

21. Goalie, is a net "M"

23. NHL Penguins LW #43 Danton "H"

24. Norfolk Admi___, Hurricanes ECHL affl team

25. KY Derby winning horse Go For "G" ate from Stanley Cup, 1994

28. Hockey HOF ind. 1993, (C) Edgar Lap___

30. 1980-1990s "Nintendo Entertainment System" - played Hockey videogames

31. Player complained to ref, was ___ off

32. NHL Avalanche LW #37 J.T. "C"

33. "A stadium" for hockey AKA

34. Concession food, comes w sauce

36. Negative contract reaction

37. HOF Ted Kennedy NN

38. Ret. Blue, Leaf Alexander "S" AKA Fixer

40. Superstitious playoff growths

42. Bruins David P___nak, 2020 All-Star MVP

43. 2016 Mark Messier Leadership Award, NSH

46. Team in "their" city, "their" arena

47. Bruins LW Jake DeBrusk NN

48. NHL Sharks C #18 "L" Pederson

49. Contract upping. Also a poker term

51. Canadiens 1911-12 logo letters

PUZZLE 35

Hockey Fact: On Feb 6th, 1976 Darryl Sittler of the Maple Leafs set the NHL record for most points scored in one game with 10. His 5 goals & 5 assists helped the Leafs defeat the Boston Bruins 11-4.

Across

1. CCHA = '___ Collegiate Hockey Association
7. Sabres NN
11. Not-so-good player or team
12. Rodents found in old arenas
13. CGY Saddledome AHL team, 2021
14. 2008 NHL All-Star MVP, Canes "E.S."
17. Sharks share SF Bay area w NBA W___ors
18. NHL Edmonton Oilers Province (short)
19. NHL-NHLPA Collective B___ining Agreement
20. NHL All-Star game 1998-2002, N.A. vs?
22. 4 Cup winner Chris Kunitz NN
23. To give a player a nickname
24. Fr. D, 40 career injuries, Sami "S"
25. Holds jocks onto players
28. Br___way, no D btwn player & goalie
31. "Fr. D, MTL Cpt, "Shea Michael Weber"
32. NHL Islanders LW #28 Michael "D"
33. Sport___, Canadian broadcaster of NHL
34. Fan demeanor of losing team
35. 10yr fr. ATL WPG Jim "S" AKA Slats
38. LAK 1986 1st rd pick, 2nd overall, Jimmy "C"
40. Elite Hockey Alliance
41. NHL Rangers G #31 "I" Shesterkin
43. Skate tighten action
44. NHL San Jose Sharks ___ Center, cap 18K
45. Shawn H___ff, 2008 All-Star Skills Fastest Skater winner
46. Gatorade electrolytes prevent muscle "S"
50. NHL Oilers D #6 "K" Russell
52. 90's great - "Kirk Alan McLean"
54. Check NHL.com for one (short)
55. The team "S" a lot to get the Free Agent
57. NHL Flames D #44 "E" Gudbranson
59. Hurricanes share N. Carolina w NBA H___ts
60. Penguins share Pittsburgh w MLB P___es
61. Arena ice is set at what? Celsius
63. Hockey HOF ind. 2002, (C) Bernie Fed___

64. Games played by 1972 WHA's Miami Screaming Eagles team
65. Calgary's ___growth Saddledome, 2000-10
66. Already "watched" game
67. Fr. Devils RW David Clarkson NN = Grit "G"

Down

1. Arena car hold
2. The Hockey News proof-reader
3. 90's great - "Tommy Mikael Salo"
4. EDM 1999 1st rd pick, 13th overall, Jani "R"
5. Trading - of "a player" or ___
6. MTL's Youppi, 1st mascot to switch what?
7. Hawks C Andrew "S" AKA The Mutt
8. WHA Houston team 1972–78
9. 18yr Fr NHL G Tom "B" AKA Tomcat
10. NJD 2021 1st rd pick, 29th overall, Chase "S"
11. Mocks opponent, bird slang
15. Pens Captain Sidney Crosby NN Captain "C"
16. NHL Sharks RW #62 Kevin "L"
21. NHL Capitals C #26 Nic "D"
26. Knights LW Max Pacioretty AKA "P" Ready
27. Ret. 600g now Czech politician, Jiri "S" AKA Guma
29. Hockey HOF ind. 1958, (C) Duke K
30. Traveling team is on one
35. Pros sign cards & posters with them
36. NHL Capitals C #29 Hendrix "L"
37. Don Cherry's ___ Sock'em video series
39. NHL "year" of play AKA
40. Oilers used to share EDM w CFL what? NN
42. Loud noise from fans after a goal
47. Slang term for referee
48. Don Cherry, outspokenness is one
49. Ret. Blue, Leaf Alexander "S" AKA Fixer
51. Fr. Blues G, S. Cup champ Jake Allen's NN
53. 2m penalty
56. Hockey HOF ind. 1958, (D) Red Du___
58. 4 Cup winner Chris Kunitz NN
62. Ottawa NHL player (short)

PUZZLE 36

Hockey Fact: Wayne Gretzky holds the most NHL records by any player with 61. Fun fact - because he had played in the pro league WHA before his first year in the NHL, he was not eligible for the rookie of the year Calder Trophy, maybe the only reward/record he did not win.

Across

1. Red Wings were the Fal___, 1930-32
5. Hockey HOF ind. 1982, (C) Norm Ul___
9. Slices concession food
14. Hockey HOF ind. 1950, (C) Joe Ma___
15. End to end mark made on telestrator
16. Slapshot, mascot ___ for Washington Capitals
17. Name of Wild uniform's red
19. CAR 2003 1st rd pick, 2nd overall, Eric "S"
20. Primary duty of a team's General Manager
21. Blues Oskar Sundqvist NN
22. Off-color, extreme design jerseys
23. Hockey HOF ind. 1973, (G) Chuck Ra___
25. "A stadium" for hockey AKA
29. NHL Flames G #80 Dan "V"
33. "I" Man = player on a 'games-played' streak
34. Nordiques chose to ___cate to Denver, 1995
36. Sabres, slow-derogatory NN
37. 1988 'Wayne Gretzky Hockey' VG, played on this computer "system": Abbr
38. Term "Canuck" means Canadian, this way
40. Paid to play player (short)
41. Arena's concession's is air-born
44. Arena beer option
45. HOF has six___ On-Ice Officials, as of 2020
46. Fans "absorb" a game's action
48. NHL All-Star games, all-time penalty shot success total
50. Wild G Cam Talbot NN
52. NHL Capitals RW #43 "T" Wilson
53. Capitals Head Coach Peter Lavio___
56. A Cleveland WHA player, 1972-76
62. NHL Capitals C #20 Lars "E"
63. Lower attendance arena, bathroom access
64. Name of Kraken logo eye's red
65. "Vision" to watch game
66. Oilers used to share EDM w CFL what? NN
67. 94 Ranger Olczyk, ok'd KY what? horse to eat from Stanley Cup
68. Hockey HOF ind. 1989, (LW) Herbie L___
69. Paul Newman hockey movie, '77's Slap "S"

Down

1. Sports Desk game "bit"
2. Hockey HOF ind. 1974, (LW) Dickie M___
3. Hockey HOF ind. 1988, (C) Buddy O'Co___
4. Dedicated follower of Ottawa team (short)
5. "Islanders" misspelling on Stanley Cup 1981
6. NHL Minnesota Wild State (short)
7. Stars share Dallas w the MLB R___rs
8. Cam, Bruins President
9. Blues Tyler Bozak NN, Phil "K" Chauffeur
10. Hat trick type, all in one period
11. US state Mich___ has 2 teams in the OHL
12. Fr. G Peter Budaj, had Ned___ders on mask
13. Hockey HOF ind. 2005, (RW) Cam N___
18. Lion-like noise from fan after a goal
24. Las Vegas Golden Knights State: Abbr
25. Arena concourse concession pleasantry
26. NHL Bruins LW #92 Tomas "N"
27. Hockey HOF ind. 1958, (G) Alec Con___
28. NHL Flyers Head Coach "A" Vigneault
30. Fr Pen & Wild Pascal Dupuis NN
31. Contract yes by both parties
32. HOF ind. 2008, (RW) Glenn Ande___
33. Team L___rom, 2011 All-Star Relay win
35. Player names engraved ___ the Stanley Cup
39. Referee hand "actions", non verbal comms.
42. In the middle of the Bruins 8-spoke wheel
43. Flyers nearly premiered as the "L" Bells, '66
45. Maple Leafs hot NN
47. Number (stat abbr)
49. CGY Saddledome's $98M in 1983
51. Most fans say arena hotdogs "T" great
53. Team with more goals so far has the?
54. Hockey HOF ind. 1985, (C) Jean R
55. Hockey HOF ind. 1989, (C) Darryl Sit___
57. Coach hard "grind" action. Often w gum
58. 6-team fr. goalie Dwayne Roloson NN
59. Satellite equipment to watch games
60. Fr. Gretzky protector, Dave Sem___
61. Players do on bench between shifts

PUZZLE 37

Hockey Fact: In 1969, Phil Esposito of the Boston Bruins became the 1st NHL player to record 100 points in a single season.

Across

1. A Hockey player in Montreal, NN
5. Louie the blue ___ bear of the Pittsburgh Penguins
10. Bruins Head Coach, Bruce C___dy
14. New York Rangers, ___son Square Garden
15. On the back of a hockey jersey
16. Arena entrance
17. Mascots fire them from air cannons
19. 1800s outdoor game pucks, frozen dung type
20. 3x Cup win Ret. Justin Williams NN
21. AKA bleachers
22. Coaches do with player's skills at try-outs
24. Detroit AKA "Hockeytown", a Reg. Tr___ark
26. Hockey HOF ind. 1971, (LW) Gordon Rob___
27. Trade talk, means team's ___ing moving player
31. Ticket from stub
35. EHA = ___ Hockey Alliance
36. Fr Pen & Wild Pascal Dupuis, NN
38. AHL Charlotte Checkers on the scoreboard
39. Sta___ Cup, is for the NHL Playoffs
40. 10yr 5-team LW Daniel Carcillo NN Gorilla "S"
41. YT, a streaming ___form for clips
42. NHL Senators LW #18 "T" Stützle
43. NHL Canadiens RW #73 "T" Toffoli
44. Fr. 10yr 5-team RW Dale "W" AKA Dutch Gretzky
45. NHL Red Wings D #53 Moritz "S"
47. Said if player is "wearing jock"
49. "Check" the scores in paper
51. Groups of plays AKA
52. Reason many teams relocate to new cities
56. 15yr fr. Sen, Chris Neil NN
60. Team F___no, 2015 All-Star Skills Relay win
61. New York Islanders arena, cap 17K
62. NHL Blitz game location
63. Blues Cpt Ryan O'Reilly NN
64. Guelph's OHL hockey team
66. Mouth guards are not m___tory in the NHL
67. ___avox, 1st Hockey VG maker, 1979
68. 2003 Jennings Trophy Winner, PHI
69. Hockey HOF ind. 2011, (C) Joe Nieuwe___

Down

1. Broadcaster audio equipment need
2. NHL MVP award
3. Atlanta Gl___tors, Ottawa Sens ECHL affl
4. Fr Coyote LW Paul Bissonnette's NN
5. Puck went from one player to another
6. NHL Ottawa Senators Province: Abbr
7. Lightning's St. Pete Times Forum NN, The Ice Pa___
8. Coyotes are threatening one, again in 2021
9. Stanley Cup is "R" yearly to playoff champ
10. Coach does when strategy fails
11. Concession drink option
12. SHL = ___hern Hockey League
13. Arturs "I", '1999 All-Star Breakaway (saves)
18. LW/D Gerard, 1 of 9 first members of HOF
23. Hockey HOF ind. 1974, (D) Art Cou___
25. CAN won a gold one at 2002 Olympics
27. Thousands needed to buy ticket
28. 14yr Capitals G, Olaf Kolzig NN
29. Fr. Shark, Pen, G Antii "N" AKA Nemo
30. Guidelines AKA
32. SportCenter will show what? of a game
33. NHL Avalanche goal-song, ___ the Sun
34. S.I.'s Farber, named the Leafs as most what? NHL team
37. Plastic, foam, and strap, are to a helmet
40. Tampa Bay Lightning AHL affl "S" Crunch
41. Pepsi Center NN, Denver (Avs)
43. Hockey HOF has six___ On-Ice Officials as members, as of 2020
44. Ice surface before it is frozen
46. NYR alt. Cpt Mika Zibanejad NN
48. From QC Nordiques to Avalanche, 1995
50. Jagr's 950K gambling, 1998-2002
52. YT, a streaming plat___ for clips
53. NHL Coyotes D #46 "I" Lyubushkin
54. Tampa Bay NHL team NN
55. World Hockey A___iation, 1971-79
57. Capitals state of play, Mary___, pre 1997
58. Habs Joel Edmunson NN
59. 2002 movie Slap Shot 2: B___ing the Ice
65. Roller Hockey

PUZZLE 38

Hockey Fact: 4x Cup winner, 17yr player Craig MacTavish was the last player in the NHL to play without a helmet when he retired in 1997.

Across

1. Mario Lemieux played while being treated for Lymp___
5. Rangers Mike R___er, 1994 All-Star MVP
9. NHL Blues LW #20 Brandon "S"
13. A team's G___al Manager deals w trades
14. "Peanuts! Beer!" - heard from afar
16. Hockey HOF ind. 1985, (C) Jean Rat___
17. Hockey HOF ind. 2020, (RW) Jarome Ig___
18. How flag is shown on NHL jersey
19. Eastern Conf. = Prince of W___, pre 1993
20. Pro calls it quits due to age
22. Guy "H" won '97 All-Star Breakaway (saves)
24. "TV" satellite company, carries sports
26. "USA, USA, USA"
27. NHL Flames D #8 Christopher "T"
30. NHL Jets LW #80 Pierre-Luc "D"
32. Don Cherry's suits, often ___eous
34. 90's great - "Brian Edward Bellows"
35. On what most fans watch the game
39. 80's great - "Mark Steven Howe"
40. NHL Panthers LW #94 Ryan "L"
43. Score more than opponent, result
44. Check NHL.com for one (short)
46. Cap Cpt Alex Ovechkin NN
47. Police do with unruly fans at the game
49. Home team did for Visiting team
52. Sharks share San Jose w MLS "E" Quakes
53. Turn___, post w arms entering arena
55. Canadian teams in the NHL
57. Scored on "unattended goal"
59. Fits inside a hockey glove
63. 2002 movie - Slap Shot 2: B___ing the Ice
64. 17yr Fr. C Scott Gomez NN
66. Hockey HOF ind. 1963, (D) Harry Cam___
67. Package of 12 pucks
68. NHL did, for a Boston franchise in 1924
69. Backup goalie will w bench most games (slang)
70. Kings share L.A. w the NBA L___s
71. Numbers that gamblers want to know
72. Fan plants their butt here

Down

1. How some became team owners
2. Hockey HOF ind. 1992, (C) Marcel Di___
3. Cheese action, overtop of concession nachos
4. A NYC WHA player, 1972-73
5. NHL - WHA merger had a D___sal draft
6. Team did like a dog & stick, for playoff birth
7. Team is "on-fire"
8. NHL Golden Knights RW #89 Alex "T"
9. Cam Neely's trucker char - Dumb & Dumber
10. NHL Canadiens G #34 Jake "A"
11. Kraken eye in the logo, name of red used
12. Har___ Shot, All-Star Skills Comp. event
15. Sens C Chris Tierney NN
21. Maple Leafs are to the Canadiens
23. Roller Hockey International
25. Hawks share Chicago w MLB what? NN
27. Flyers AHL affl Lehigh Valley Phan___
28. AIHF = ___ralian Ice Hockey Federation
29. Hockey HOF ind. 1960, (D) Sylvio Ma___
31. 1975-79 WHA Cincinnati Stingers logo
33. Final score is "zero" (slang)
36. Hockey HOF ind. 1976, (G) Johnny B___
37. Bump type after a goal
38. Hurricanes share N. Carolina w NFL P___ers
41. (Ret.) 11 season "Marty Vincent Turco"
42. Canadiens in 1910-11 logo was this color Maple Leaf
45. HOF G Ken Dryden NN
48. 1940 Stanley Cup winner, New York
50. 90's great - "Owen Liam Nolan"
51. Last yrs Stanley Cup winners are the ___ing champs
53. Booth announcers do it for a living
54. 1977 movie 'Slap Shot', final scene exposure AKA Strip what?
56. Fr. Canuck Jake Virtanen NN
57. Canucks logo, AKA whale
58. Toronto WHA player, 1973-76
60. Great Lake Detroit Red Wings are near
61. Hockey HOF ind. 1967, (G) Turk B___
62. Sport___, Canadian broadcaster of NHL
65. Ret. Pens C Maxime Talbot NN "M" Max

PUZZLE 39

Hockey Fact: While Canadiens goalie Jacques Plante is credited with creation of the "modern" goalie mask having worn one during a game in 1959, Clint Benedict also wore a leather mask for 5 games in 1930 with the NHL Montreal Maroons. Benedict was also a pro lacrosse goalie.

Across

1. Fans do among those sitting near & online
5. 2002 Olympics "Salt" locale, CAN wins gold
9. Periods, eras or ___ in hockey
13. NHL Kings' Training facility, formerly Health ___ Training Center
14. Ottawa Senators logo, Roman Gen___
15. Player must dress this way, pre game arrival
16. NHL Senators C #12 Shane "P"
17. WCHA = Western ___egiate Hockey Assoc.
18. Hockey HOF ind. 1978, (G) Jacques Pl___
19. 1974 All-Star MVP, Blues Garry "U"
20. An arena ice what? is 3/4 inch thick
22. Hockey HOF ind. 1963, (F) Shorty G___
23. "Burner" game, lots of goals scored
24. Sharks share San Jose w MLS "E" Quakes
27. Oiler alt. Cpt Leon Draisaitl NN
29. Newer arena, restaurant level descriptor
31. Press consensus best NHL #4, Bobby "O"
32. 2016 Lady Byng Trophy Winner, LAK
33. Goalies pads are like a knight's "A"
36. ___ce, protects your team's end
37. Minor back injury description
39. Ticket seat info (short)
40. Crowd grows "H" after continual bad calls
41. ANA 2006 1st rd pick, 19th overall Mark "M"
45. EHA = ___ Hockey Alliance
46. Sami K___en, 2000 All-Star Fastest Skater
48. "Top" team, or top player AKA
50. Ticket numbers $old counts as what?
52. Fr. 10yr 5-team RW Dale "W" AKA Dutch Gretzky
53. Fits inside hockey glove
56. Satellite equipment to watch games
57. NHL Canadiens RW #40 Joel "A"
58. Hockey HOF ind. 1975, (LW) Ace Ba___
59. Eastern Conf. was Pr___ of Wales, pre '93
60. Ret. 600g now Czech politician, Jiri "S" AKA Guma
61. Acco___'s 'Brett Hull Hockey' VG 1993

Down

1. Toy Story's Don Rickles ___ the term "Don't be a Hockey Puck"
2. Concession food solves it
3. At live game
4. Ret. enforcer Chris Thorburn NN
5. Ret. 16yr John "L", AKA Johnny Vermont
6. A lion-like reaction from a fan
7. NHL Blackhawks D #48 Wyatt "K"
8. Hockey HOF ind. 1985, (C) Jean Rat___
9. NHL Anaheim Ducks on the scoreboard
10. NHL team will/does, for city revenue
11. 94 Ranger Olczyk, ok'd KY Derby horse to what? from Stanley Cup
12. NHL Red Wings D #70 Troy "S"
13. Common bone / spinal hockey injury
21. Producing players earn it from fans
23. Stanley Cup shape resembles this type "drum"
25. Kings play in the P___ic Division
26. Bruins play in the A___tic Division
28. First year players
30. 2001 Clancy Trophy Winner, Colorado
33. Miss practice, unexpectedly, no reason: Abbr
34. Coach chose not to coach anymore
35. NHL Capitals D #52 "M" Irwin
37. Philip's Arena NN, Thrashers 1999-2011
38. Contract negotiating. Also, passing out cards
39. Puck "damaged" above board glass
42. NHL Kraken RW #7 Jordan "E"
43. NHL Sharks G #47 James "R"
44. To "place" in a position, or to the minors
47. NHL Hurricanes D #22 Brett "P"
49. Uniform wear and what?
51. Atlanta Gl___tors, Ottawa Sens ECHL affl
52. Glove palm to opponents = face what?
54. 90's great - "Anthony Lewis Amonte"
55. Hockey HOF ind. 1970, (RW) Babe "D"

62. Old arenas like CGY Saddledome haven't done it well
63. Oilers, most Nort___ of any NHL team

PUZZLE 40

Hockey Fact: Goalies cannot handle, carry, or even contact/touch the puck on the opposite side of the center line. Doing so incurs a penalty.

Across

1. NHL Kraken D #6 "A" Larsson
5. TB G Brian Elliot NN
9. Concession soda tool
14. Past NHL All-Star player selection by fan "V"
15. Don Cherry story "___ Your Head Up Kid"
16. "Volume" of the broadcasted game AKA
17. NHL maps each franchise their own "A"
18. Capitals share D.C. w the MLB what? NN
19. Wilds Mats Zuccarello NN
20. NHL TV blackout rules
22. Roch Carrier 'wrote' "The Hockey Sweater"
23. Anthem, where you place your hand
25. CBC' "B" of the Blades, Hky + Figure Skaters
29. "Bruin", from "R" the Fox tale, means Brown
34. A Oakland NHL player, 1967-76
35. J. Sakic, un___ited in Sandler's Happy Gilmore
37. Gordie Howe died in Sylvania "O", 2016
38. Bruins D Charlie McAvoy NN
39. Fr. MTL Maroons NN
40. VAN 1980 1st round pick, 10th overall, Rick
41. Package of 12 pucks
42. OHL = ___rio Hockey League
43. NHL Devils LW #59 "J" Kuokkanen
44. All-Star game 1998-2002, World vs North "A"
46. 1970 Stanley Cup Champion Coach, BOS
47. Predators NN - Dorktown "C"
50. First game of season AKA
54. 2005 CBA, player salaries did, by 24%
59. NHL Sharks D #51 Simek
60. HOF G Grant Fuhr NN
61. Sami K___en, 2000 All-Star Skills Fastest Skater
62. Bruins logo, an eight "S" wheel
63. Fr Hab, Flyer Eric Desjardins NN
64. Coach's tip, sometimes written in a book
65. Cleveland NHL player, 1976-78
66. Hockey HOF ind. 1959, (G) Tiny Thom___
67. "Happy" fans. Also, TV show w dancing

Down

1. John T___es, 2016 All-Star Skills Shot Accuracy
2. 1987 'Hat Trick' game on the Commo___ 64
3. Hockey HOF ind. 2012, (C) Adam O___
4. NHL pre-game tailgating entree
5. Sharks Evander Kane NN
6. 1980 NHL All-Star MVP, Flyers Reggie "L"
7. Capitals Head Coach Peter Lavio___
8. 80's great - "Stanley Philip Smyl"
9. Flyers 1981-83 Cooperall pants, banned for?
10. Arena bathroom queue, wait your "T"
11. Hockey HOF ind. 1966, (D) Ken Rea___
12. G Knights share Vegas w the NFL R___rs
13. NHL Devils LW #44 Miles "W"
21. RH = ___er Hockey (league)
22. Predators NN
24. Hockey game place
25. Sharks Alt. Cpt, Brent Burns NN Chew___
26. Press consensus best NHL #45, Aaron "A"
27. Slap Shot movie final scene exposure AKA Strip?
28. Hawks Cpt Jonathan Toews NN
30. Owen "N", drafted 1990 by QC Nordiques
31. Fits inside a hockey glove
32. 2021 Clancy Trophy Winner, Nashville
33. Average pucks used per game
35. Stanley Cup visited Late Night w "O'Brien"
36. Old arenas moldy condition
39. Bruins first owner Adams was g___ magnate
43. Protects female hockey player's groin region
45. NYR ECHL affl JAX team
46. Old West sports pub
48. AHL Lions play in ___ Rivieras QC
49. NHL Predators RW #23 Grimaldi
50. Peter F___erg, '98 All-Star Skills Shot Accuracy
51. Peter Stastny is to Paul Stastny
52. Sergei F___ov, 92 All-Star Skills Fastest Skater
53. NHL Blues D #77 Mikkola
55. Pens alt. Cpt Kris Letang NN
56. N___eon replica cannon fired at CBJ games
57. Nordiques chose to relo___ to Denver 1995
58. Injury forced Bobby Orr's retirement, '78
60. 90's great - "Christopher Robert Pronger"

PUZZLE 41

1	2	3	4		5	6	7	8		9	10	11	12	13
14					15					16				
17					18					19				
20				21					22					
			23				24							
25	26	27	28					29			30	31	32	33
34					35	36					37			
38				39							40			
41				42						43				
44				45					46					
			47			48	49							
50	51	52	53				54				55	56	57	58
59					60						61			
62					63						64			
65					66						67			

Hockey Fact: NA Pro hockey rink ice is ¾ of an inch (1.9cm) thick & is kept at a temp. of 16 degrees Fahrenheit (-9 degrees Celsius).

Across

1. SCHC = ___cuse Crunch Hockey Club
5. KHL = ___inental Hockey League
9. NY is to the Sabres
14. Hurricanes Eric S___, 2008 All-Star MVP
15. Fr. G Eddie 'The Eagle' B___ur
16. Final scores, added up
17. 1990s NHL Breakway VG series by ___aim
18. Hockey HOF ind. 1958, (G) Alec Con___
19. Bernie P___, left NHL for WHA year 1
20. Ret. Bruin G Tim Thomas NN
22. Kings owner "E.R."
24. Slang term for referees
25. Mark made on telestrator
26. Slap Shot, a Sport Co___ movie
27. Don Cherry's playing career w Bruins
32. QC Nordiques owners Carling O'Keefe Br___
34. Switched teams
35. "Cut" from team
36. Arena money giver: Abbr
37. Traditional Defenceman AKA ___ home
41. Owner puts it on coach after loss
44. HOF ind. 2001, (RW) Mike "G" (CAN)
46. How some became team owners
47. Timothy Leif Oshie (T. J.)
48. Miami Arena NN, Panthers
52. HOF G Billy Smith NN = "H" Man
56. MTL missed the playoffs 1943-67
57. Stars ECHL Affl. Steelheads
58. HOF ind. 2003, (C) Pat LaFont___ (US)
60. TB Lightening Girls, dance "U" until 2019
61. Ret. 10yr Hab Chris "N" AKA Knuckles
62. Hockey HOF ind. 1989, (C) Darryl Sit___
63. "Maple Leaf" was owner Smythe's WW1 ___ment
64. Arena fries - why you need a soda after
65. Oilers share Edmonton w the CFL what?
66. Penguins share Pittsburgh w the MLB P___es

Down

1. Check NHL.com for them (short)
2. Hawks, 1st team to sound horn after goal, and their first horn type was from what?
3. Indy WHA player, 1974-78
4. Gretzky, the Greatest Of what?
5. HOF ind. 1966, (C) Ted "K" (CAN)
6. Fr. Pen, Cap D, Steven "O" AKA Binky
7. Bruins in "NHL", Patriots in the what?
8. Wings Affl, ECHL Walleye Ohio city
9. Flyers G Carter Hart AKA "S" Hart
10. Toronto WHA player, 1973-76
11. Hockey HOF ind. 2012, (C) Adam O___
12. Ret. Bruin G Tim Thomas NN
13. NBA C___cs ran the Bruins org. 1951-64
21. 1990s enforcer Stu Grimson AKA The Grim Re___
23. Toy Story's Rickles "___ be a Hockey Puck"
28. General Admission
29. NHL Rangers D #23 "A" Fox
30. NHL Senators D #98 Victor "M"
31. NHL Edmonton Oilers on the scoreboard
32. Penguins GM Ron H___ll
33. Hockey card graders look for "W" & tear
35. 90's great - "Adam Scott Graves"
38. Stream platform, for games & clips: Abbr
39. NHL Panthers LW #10 "A" Duclair
40. "Vision" to watch game
41. Bruins NN
42. Arena beer option
43. NHL Canadiens LW #62 "A" Lehkonen
45. Entrance turn stile motion
46. NHL Red Wings D #17 Filip "H"
49. Hockey HOF ind. 1962, (LW) Sweeney Sch___
50. 1988 'Wayne Gretzky Hockey' VG on "A"
51. VAN '82 1st rd pick, 11th overall, Michel "P"
52. Panthers share Miami w the NFL Dolp___
53. Atlanta Gl___tors, Ottawa Sens ECHL affl
54. Regulation net is 4 feet
55. NHL Sub-Reddit action
59. NHL Chicago Blackhawks State (short)

PUZZLE 42

1	2	3	4		5	6	7	8		9	10	11	12	13
14					15					16				
17					18					19				
20				21			22	23						
24						25								
			26				27			28	29	30	31	
	32	33						34						
35											36			
37			38	39	40			41	42	43				
44					45		46							
			47				48				49	50	51	
52	53	54	55				56							
57					58	59				60				
61				62					63					
64				65					66					

Hockey Fact: The first $1M dollar contract in NHL history was in 1971 when the Boston Bruins signed Bobby Orr to a five-year deal worth $200,000 per season.

Across

1. Rangers share "New York" w NFL Gi___

5. NHL Predators D #59 "R" Josi

10. EA Sports NHL series is soft___

14. Capitals state of play was ___land, pre 1997

15. 1980s US VG console maker w Hockey games

16. Carl H___in, 2012 All-Star Skills Fastest Skater

17. Coyotes alt. Cpt Phil Kessel NN

19. 90's great - "Raymond Garfield Sheppard"

20. 33rd pick 2005, James "___ Deal" Neal

21. NHL Hurricanes D #74 Jaccob "S"

22. NHL Sabres G #31 Dustin "T"

24. Stars share Dallas w the NBA M___icks

26. Goalies keep puck from the net

27. Ottawa Senators logo, from Roman Empire

31. NHL Panthers goal-song

35. NHL Rangers LW #91 Sammy "B"

36. Fr Pen & Wild Pascal Dupuis NN

38. KY Derby winning horse Go For "G" ate from Stanley Cup, 1994

39. Fr. enforcer Derek "Boogie Man" B___ard

40. Short distance, near-net goal AKA

41. Stanley Cup visited Russert's "___ the Press"

42. Arena "level" (short)

43. Don Cherry, 3_ years on Coach's Corner

44. NHL Senators C #12 Shane "P"

45. HOF Ted Kennedy NN

47. Penguins AHL Affl Penguins in "S" PA

49. Ticket scanning gun noise

51. NHL Predators RW #28 "E" Tolvanen

52. Kraken logo eye color

56. Puck went from one player to another

60. NHL Blue Jackets LW #50 "E" Robinson

61. NHL 2K VG, on this motion-control console

62. Erie's OHL hockey team

63. Hypertext on NHL.com

64. A Dallas NHL player

66. Fr. Gretzky protector, Dave Sem___

67. Goalie's 5-hole. Puck goes through what?

68. NYR alt Cpt Artemi Panarin NN

69. Hockey HOF ind. 2008, (RW) Glenn Ande___

Down

1. Broadcaster audio equipment need

2. North American Hockey League

3. NHL Wild's Training facility, ___ Rink

4. Gordie Howe's died in this Ohio city, 2016

5. HOF ind. 1973, (G) Chuck "R" (CAN)

6. Extra session of play: Abbr

7. Avs owners also own Wal___ dept store chain

8. Leafs share Toronto w the CFL what? NN

9. DAL 2005 1st rd pick, 28th overall, Matt "N"

10. NHL Oilers LW #37 "W" Foegele

11. Periods, eras or "A" in hockey

12. 2002's Slap Shot 2: B___ing the Ice

13. Hockey HOF ind. 2010, (RW) Dino Ciccar___

18. Hockey Wives' Reality TV, shows their daily?

23. John T___es, 2016 All-Star Skills Shot Accuracy

25. Blues Cpt Ryan O'Reilly NN

27. A Tampa Bay player, NN

28. Hockey goalies use it to catch pucks

29. Slapshot, the ___ mascot of the Capitals

30. Ret. Leaf Joffrey Lupul NN

32. The "A" in FA (status)

33. NHL Sharks LW #83 Matt "N"

34. NHL Senators G #31 "A" Forsberg

37. Concession pizza portion

40. Trade, involving more than 2 parties/teams

41. HOF G Ken Dryden, '04 Liberal Cabinet "M"

43. Penguins share Pittsburgh w the NFL S___ers

44. NHL Lightning LW #18 Ondrej "P"

46. Coyotes share Arizona w MLB what? NN

48. Sports writers job

50. NHL St. Louis Blues Enter ___ Center

52. Hockey HOF ind. 1965, (F) Arthur Far___

53. Great Lake Detroit Red Wings are near

54. Concession till noise

55. Preds share Nashville with the NFL ___ns

57. Senators NN

58. Hockey HOF ind. 2002, (C) Bernie Fed___

59. Hu___ river divides the Devils - Rangers

65. Sharks share SF Bay area w MLB OAK what?

PUZZLE 43

¹	²	³	⁴	■	⁵	⁶	⁷	⁸	⁹	■	¹⁰	¹¹	¹²	¹³
¹⁴				■	¹⁵					■	¹⁶			
¹⁷				¹⁸		■	¹⁹			■	²⁰			
²¹						■	²²			²³				
■	■		²⁴			²⁵	■	²⁶				■	■	■
²⁷	²⁸	²⁹				■	³⁰	■	³¹			³²	³³	³⁴
³⁵					■	³⁶		³⁷			■	³⁸		
³⁹				■	⁴⁰					■	⁴¹			
⁴²			■	⁴³				■	⁴⁴				
⁴⁵			⁴⁶			■	⁴⁷		⁴⁸				
■	■		⁴⁹			⁵⁰	■	⁵¹			■	■	■
⁵²	⁵³	⁵⁴				⁵⁵	■	⁵⁶			⁵⁷	⁵⁸	⁵⁹
⁶⁰			■	⁶¹			■	⁶²				
⁶³			■	⁶⁴		⁶⁵		■	⁶⁶			
⁶⁷			■	⁶⁸				■	⁶⁹			

Hockey Fact: The 1st NHL goal was scored in the 1ˢᵗ period at exactly 1:00 on Dec. 19, 1917 by Dave Ritchie of the Montreal Wanderers against the Toronto Arenas. Ritchie scored the last goal of the game, the team's 10ᵗʰ and game winner as Montreal won 10-9.

Across

1. All-Star Skills Comp. event, "H" shot
7. Ret. Leaf Joffrey Lupul NN
12. A contract come-again
13. 8th pick 2005, fr Shark Devin Setoguchi NN
14. Blue Jackets NN
17. Canucks Brock Bo___, 2018 All-Star MVP
18. Tops arena drink
19. Ontario Hockey Association
21. 90's great - "Keith Matthew Tkachuk"
22. EDM 1989 1st rd pick, 15th overall, Jason "S"
26. Free place after contract expires
28. St. Louis Blues ___prise Center, cap 19K
29. NAHL = ___ American Hockey League
30. 1990s NHL Breakway VG series by Acc___
31. Concession food pricing, most NHL arenas
34. Napoleon rep___ cannon fired at Blue Jackets games
35. Losing teams pray to him for better fortune
36. 2005 CBA, player salaries ro___ back by 24%
38. NYI ECHL affl team in Worcester Mass.
41. Stanley Cup visited Jay on The Tonight Show
42. NHL Stars C #12 "R" Faksa
43. Blues alt Cpt Vladimir Tarasenko NN
44. NHL Panthers G #72 "S" Bobrovsky
45. NHL Maple Leafs RW #16 Mitchell "M"
46. Paid to play player (short)
48. Hockey player in Ottawa (short)
49. $ offer for players services
50. Hockey HOF ind. 1974, (LW) Dickie M___
52. Ret. Leafs Cpt Dion Phaneuf NN Sloppy "S"
55. Damaged uniform
56. Tix info, age descriptor
57. 26th pick 1987, G Rick Tabaracci NN = Hot Dog "S"

Down

2. 80's great - "Randolph Robert Carlyle"
3. Contract negotiator. Also, Vegas card person
4. NHL Senators RW #63 Tyler "E"
5. Down to Farm League
6. # of Michigan teams in the OHL
8. ___ a stick for shottong, scoring
9. Senators NN "P" Sens
10. ANA 2010 1st rd pick, 29th overall, Emerson
11. Stat column organization
15. Detach stub before game, result
16. 1974 Stanley Cup Champion Coach, PHI
20. Hurricanes share N. Carolina w NFL P___ers
22. Owner wants to get rid of team, action
23. TV station status when reporting on game
24. Devils AHL Comets city
25. Hockey HOF ind. 1984, (C) Jacques "L"
26. VAN 1990 1st rd pick, 18th overall, Shawn "A"
27. Sabres D Colin Miller NN
32. NHL Flames C #42 Gawdin
33. 15yr NYR G, Henrik Lundqvist NN
35. NHL Islanders D #4 Andy "G"
37. Fans enter through it, into arena
39. Caps Nicklas Backstrom NN, Star "L"
40. All 4 are checked by hockey card grader
43. Calgary's Scotiabank "S" dome
44. Reaction to fans after bad season
45. Arena ice is set at "M" 9 Celsius
46. Banged after a win, ___ & pans
47. Fan support for team. Also, tree part
49. A common type of check
51. 90's great - "Erik Nicklas Lidström"
53. NHL Islanders RW #15 "C" Clutterbuck
54. NHL St. Louis Blues on the scoreboard

58. BOS 2021 1st rd pick, 21st overall, Fabian "L"

PUZZLE 44

Hockey Fact: The newly formed NHL of 1917 consisted of only 4 teams - Montreal Canadiens, Ottawa Senators, Montreal Wanderers and Toronto Arenas.

Across

1. Popular team-store merchandise
5. Bruins 3rd jersey letter "B" design
11. 50-50 tix often supports a local "C"
12. Don Cherry, loud & outspoken, may lack?
14. NHL Penguins LW #43 "D" Heinen
15. Kraken, being in Seattle
16. Concession hot-dog bitter chopped topping
17. Hockey HOF ind. 2009, (D) Brian Le___ (US)
18. NHL Islanders LW #27 Anders "C"
19. 80's great - "Michael Anthony Foligno"
20. Ret. 17yr Wing Henrik Zetterberg NN
21. NHL.com website, underlined mark-up text
22. Sportswriter double-check
24. Mexican food concession offering
25. Fr. Canuck, twin, Daniel Sedin NN
26. 20yr Devil Ken Daneyko NN
27. Australian Roller Hockey
28. Crowds for winning teams
29. Hockey HOF ind. 2004, (D) Larry Mu___
31. Panthers and Lightning tree type (Florida)
32. Spins w puck control, spin ___
34. Mid week game night (short)
35. Modern and pre-modern pro hockey "E"
39. NHL app, on this phone
40. Texas League (1946-2020) status
41. Sutters Brent, Brian, Darryl, Duane, "R", Ron
42. NHL Kings Head Coach "T" McLellan
43. Red Wings known as Cou___, pre 1930
44. NHL Chicago Blackhawks on scoreboard
45. 90's great - "Erik Nicklas Lidström"
46. Thrashers Dany H___ey, 2003 All-Star MVP
47. Arena food mouth wiper
50. "The Hockey Sweater", short film, descriptor
52. 26yr NHLer Chris Chelios NN
53. NHL Kraken RW #72 Joonas "D"
54. Dirty players are "H" by all, even teammates
55. Given to the greats at HOF
56. WHA Los Angeles team, 1972

Down

1. NHL Flames D #55 Noah "H"
2. Pro player operates an expensive one
3. Hockey HOF ind. 1994, (LW) Harry Wa___
4. Ottawa NHL team (short)
5. Canadiens attachment to Flanders Fields poem
6. Sharks Alt. Cpt, Brent Burns NN Chew___
7. Ligue Nord-Americaine re Hockey
8. NHL Toronto Maple Leafs Province (short)
9. NHL Canucks goal-song, Gold on the "C"
10. Avalanche owner, Ann Walton "K"
11. HNIC = Hockey Night In ___
13. Bruins LW Jake DeBrusk NN
14. Indoor play, related to arena structure
15. 1980 NHL All-Star MVP, Flyers Reggie "L"
20. NHL Flames C #47 Connor "Z"
21. Press consensus best NHL #28, Steve "L"
23. Blues D Torey Krug NN
24. Texas Amateur Hockey Association
25. NHL Islanders LW #28 Michael "D"
28. Acco___'s 'Brett Hull Hockey' VG 1993
30. 90's great - "Patrick Michael LaFontaine"
31. Penguins NN
32. NHL Avalanche RW #25 Logan "O"
33. Middle of the ice marking
34. The "W" in WHA, 1971-79
36. Comedian Don who? coined "Don't be a Hockey Puck"
37. "The Hockey Sweater" short story character
38. Cold weather hockey, pick up games
40. Ticket seat info description
42. Hockey HOF ind. 1985, (LW) Bert Olms___
43. Ret. fr Oiler Cpt Jason Smith NN
46. Br___way, no defense btwn player & goalie
47. Northern Collegiate Hockey Association
48. Amateur Hockey Association of Canada
49. Former mascot of the Pittsburgh Penguins
51. "Madison Square Garden" usually said as?

PUZZLE 45

Hockey Fact: The NHL expanded from 6 teams to 12 in 1967, the largest expansion in pro sports history. Along with the Original 6, the NHL added the California Seals, L.A. Kings, Minnesota North Stars, Philadelphia Flyers, Pittsburgh Penguins & St. Louis Blues.

Across

1. All-Star Skills Comp. event, "H" shot
7. Coaches helper (short)
11. NHL 2K VG, Apple devices, software
12. World League of Professional Hockey
13. American Hockey Coaches Association
14. High up arena seat, physical risk
17. Flyers G Carter Hart NN
18. Spins w puck control, ___ o rama
19. Leafs and Marlies (AHL) city
20. NHL Canadiens RW #40 Joel
22. Fas___ Skater, All-Star Skills Comp. event
23. 90's great - "Kirk Alan McLean"
24. NYR AHL Hartford Wolf "P"
25. Paints hockey portraits
28. Bobby Orr shoots
31. NHL Islanders LW #27 Anders "L"
32. CGY Saddledome renamed to CAN ___ lines '94
33. Hockey HOF ind. 1963, (C) Ebbie Goodfe___
34. 90's great - "Teppo Kalevi Numminen"
35. Ret. stand-up G Kirk "M" AKA Mack
38. FLA 2004 1st rd pick, 7th overall, Rostislav "O"
40. NHL Islanders GM, "L" Lamoriello
41. NHL Sharks LW #63 Jeffrey "V"
43. Panthers franchise awarded, 10th of what? 1992 (short)
44. 80's - "Igor Nikolayevich Larionov" (USSR)
45. Hockey HOF ind. 1985, (C) Jean "R"
46. 20yr RW, Blues A. coach Steve Thomas NN
50. Bruins David P___nak, 2020 All-Star MVP
52. (Ret.) Shane Albert Doan
54. Stars ECHL Affl. I___ Steelheads
55. Fr. Flame Fleury's minor pro baseball games
57. 3x Cup, Ret. G C. Osgood AKA Wizard ___
59. In front of goalie, between FO circles
60. Ottawa Senators logo, Roman Gen___
61. NHL San Jose Sharks fd. in 19__
63. Apply a number to a player's skill
64. Legend Jaromir Jagr's league locale (short)
65. "Nintendo Ent. System" - played Hockey VGs
66. HOF ind. 2015, (D) Phil Hou___ (US)
67. Press articles AKA

Down

1. HOF ind. 1963, (F) Tom H (CAN)
2. Gretzky, pro hockey's top "A" producer
3. 80's great - "Donald William Beaupre"
4. TB G Brian Elliot NN
5. Booth announcers do it for a living
6. HFD Whalers Civic Center NN, 1975-97
7. American Amputee Hockey Association
8. 2011 NHL All-Star MVP, Hawks Patrick "S"
9. NHL Coyotes C #8 Nick "S"
10. FLA 2002 1st rd pick, 9th overall, Petr "T"
11. Stanley Cup 51.4K followers on "I" (short)
15. New Jersey Devils Prud___ Center, cap 17K
16. NHL Jets D #2 Dylan "D"
21. The Kr___, Seattle's NHL team
26. Goalie that let's in goals like perforated tool
27. Behind in score
29. A broke team, likely result
30. Online support post for team
35. Blue Jackets Cleveland AHL Affl
36. Canadiens, a "C" part of French Canada
37. NHL Jets D #62 "N" Nogier
39. 2x Cup wins, Fr D, Rob Scuderi NN
40. NHL Kings C #17 "L" Andersson
42. Maple Leafs NN
47. Hockey HOF ind. 1950, (C) Joe "M"
48. NHL app, on these mobiles
49. Coyotes NN
51. Devils alte___ uniforms have green pants
53. Kraken C Ryan Donato NN
56. Hockey HOF ind. 1966, (C) Max Ben___
58. Scoreboard display with no goals
62. AHL Toronto Marlies on the scoreboard

PUZZLE 46

Hockey Fact: The NHL had no expansion between 1942 - 1967, also known as the 25 year "Original-6" era - Montreal Canadiens, Toronto Maple Leafs, Boston Bruins, New York Rangers, Detroit Red Wings & Chicago Blackhawks.

Across

1. NHL Islanders D #24 "S" Mayfield
6. Coyotes share Arizona w MLB what? NN
11. NHL Flames D #8 Christopher "T"
12. Spangled Banner
14. Highlight Of The Night - Sports Center
16. Hockey HOF ind. 1963, (F) Shorty G___
17. NHL Predators RW #28 "E" Tolvanen
18. 1950 Stanley Cup Champion Coach, DET
19. A Oakland NHL player, 1967-76
21. Hockey HOF ind. 1967, (C) Neil Colv___
22. Ret. 13yr 7-team Jaroslav Spacek NN
23. NHL Maple Leafs RW #24 "W" Simmonds
24. NHL Hurricanes D #25 Ethan "B"
25. Fr. Duck, Jet Finnish Flash, Teemu S___ne
26. Quit the game of hockey due to age
28. Fr. Canes D Niclas Wallin NN = "S" Weapon
30. AHL San Diego Gulls on the scoreboard
31. Slap Shot, a S__-Comedy movie
33. A Denver NHL player
34. Thrown on the ice at a Red Wings game
37. NHL Lightning D #52 "C" Foote
39. Krakens Brandon Tanev NN
40. NHL Boston Bruins State: Abbr
42. Fans do it with signs
45. Same score after 3 periods
47. Nachos nutritional unit (short)
48. Known agitator player, AKA
50. Concession rule, usually 2-beer
52. HOF ind. 2017, (RW) Teemu Sel___ (Fin)
53. NHL-NHLPA Collective Bargaining A___ment
54. Buffalo NHL player
55. Blues Garry U___, 1974 NHL All-Star MVP
56. Dallas Stars ___ican Airlines Center, cap 19K
57. 80's great - "Brian Louis Allen Sutter"
58. Hockey HOF ind. 1990, (C) Gilbert Perre___
59. NHL Minnesota Wild State (short)
60. 17yr 5-team RW Bill "F" AKA Cowboy

Down

1. Concession soda tool
2. Detroit Red Wings Little "C" Arena, cap 20K
3. Fr Bruin Carl Soderberg NN ___ Swede
4. The Flames are to the CGY Saddledome
5. "Hockey Wives" is a reality what? show (short)
6. NHL Ducks Head Coach "D" Eakins
7. 2007 NHL All-Star MVP, Sabres Daniel "B"
8. 20yr 5-team Jason "C" AKA Chim Dawg
9. NYR 1991 1st rd pick, 15th overall, Alexei "K"
10. Traditional Defenceman AKA "S" at home
12. Hockey HOF ind. 1961, (C) Oliver S
13. "Vision" to watch game
15. Napoleon replica ca___ fired at CBJ games
20. Wild owner Craig "L"
27. AHL Rochester Americans on the scoreboard
29. MTL '87 1st rd pick, 17th overall Andrew "C"
32. Totals (short)
35. Don Cherry's suits, "repeat" look
36. Player, team outfit (short)
37. HOF G Ken Dryden's BA degree school
38. AMHL = ___ Mens Hockey League
40. 16yr 5-team Ian Laperriere NN
41. A Pittsburgh NHL player, 1925-30
42. Do with jersey on non-game days
43. Exciting game AKA "bang ___"
44. Give the "Ok" to talk w free agent
46. Devils fan in section 122 known as?
47. CGY Saddledome renamed to ___dian Airlines 1994
49. Already watched game
51. NHL "checks" for PEDs
60. NHL Tampa Bay Lightning State: Abbr

Across (continued)

61. Fr Oiler Cpt Andrew Ference AKA Captain "P"
62. A bad team does it often

PUZZLE 47

Hockey Fact: Seattle Kraken are the latest NHL expansion team, having started in the 2021-22 season. Along with the excitement from players about their new city was the dismay/concern over the local Seattle Real Estate home prices being too high. NHL average salaries are 2.55M USD per season. Ouch!

Across

1. The team has more goals so far is in the what?
5. Player fight AKA
10. NHL Canadiens Captain "S" Weber
14. Sabres Daniel Br___, 2007 All-Star MVP
15. Jaws ___ is heard during Sharks PP
16. TSN-ESPN Ray Ferraro AKA Chicken "P"
17. NHL Senators city
19. Some arena security's day job
20. Hurricanes share N. Carolina w NBA H___ts
21. Holy game night
22. NHL network watcher
24. NHL Kings C #17 "L" Andersson
26. # of Nordiques Stanley Cups (French)
27. "Creative" modern ticket design appearance
31. Brampton ON's Campbell, fr. Hockey player, now TV analyst
35. Wild play in "S" Paul Minn.
36. Score conclusion
38. 90's great - "Patrick Michael LaFontaine"
39. Stanley Cup originally for "Dominion Hockey Chall___ Cup"
40. NHL Penguins D #4 Taylor "F"
41. Tailgating purpose, besides beer
42. KY Derby winning horse Go For Gin, ___ from Stanley Cup, 1994
43. Non winner
44. Wild uniform red color name is Iron "R"
45. Press consensus best NHL #28, Steve "L"
47. Post game question asker
49. Periods, eras or ___ in hockey
51. 1300 G, 18 Season A. Kovalev NN
52. Gambling term
56. Hockey - middle of the ice player (US sp)
60. Apple brand, game streaming device
61. 90's great - "Anthony Lewis Amonte"
62. Blues D Torey Krug NN
63. 20yr Devil Ken Daneyko NN
64. 12yr 7-team G Bob Essensa NN
66. Hockey HOF ind. 1964, (G) Bill Du___
67. Sens used to share Ottawa w CFL R___ades
68. Arena parking, "small" stall AKA
69. Fr D, 40 career injuries, Sami "S"

Down

1. HOF ind. 2013, (D) Chris Che___ (US)
2. NHL Panthers C #27 "E" Luostarinen
3. Rangers Mike G___er, 1993 All-Star MVP
4. Trades couldn't pass April 12, 2021
5. Traditional Defenceman AKA "S" at home
6. Montreal logo, lettering
7. Canadiens Mark ___hi, 1997 All-Star MVP
8. Rod Brind'___, Hurricanes Head Coach
9. Pepsi Center NN, Denver (Avs)
10. Fr. Bruins C Ryan Spooner NN
11. Helmets try to prevent it
12. NHL Red Wings LW #73 Adam "E"
13. Don Cherry, 7 seasons w Rochester ___icans
18. Nordiques uniform area w fleur de-lis x3
23. Sharks uniform core color
25. Jagr gambles a lot on web/betting what?
27. A Oakland NHL player, 1967-76
28. NHL Avalanche LW #75 Sampo "R"
29. Hamilton NHL player, 1920-25
30. EA Sports NHL game, programmer AKA
32. The team "S" a lot to get the Free Agent
33. Player depiction on trading card
34. NHL Capitals C #20 Lars "E"
37. 1999 Jennings Trophy Winner, DAL
40. Jagr did radio weather "F" to practice English
41. WHA San Diego team 1974–77
43. WCHA = Western col___ate Hockey Assoc.
44. Hockey player w no set position, 1800s
46. Ret. Devil, Sharks Ass. Coach J. Madden NN
48. Hockey uniform missing this storage thing
50. ANA 1996 1st rd pick, 9th overall Ruslan "S"
52. Goalie gloves are made from it
53. Sami K___en, 2000 All-Star Fastest Skater
54. Goal limit per period
55. Song for US teams, Star S___led Banner
57. Fr. Star, Pen, Cap Matt Niskanen NN
58. Sharks entrance song is by M___lica
59. Blues Cpt Ryan O'Reilly NN
65. Short handed, stat: Abbr

PUZZLE 48

1	2	3	4		5	6	7	8	9		10	11	12	13
14					15						16			
17				18			19				20			
21							22			23				
			24			25		26						
27	28	29					30		31			32	33	34
35						36		37				38		
39					40						41			
42				43					44					
45			46				47		48					
			49			50		51						
52	53	54				55		56			57	58	59	
60					61				62					
63					64			65			66			
67					68						69			

Hockey Fact: Frank Zamboni invented the "Zamboni", the 1st self-propelled ice-clearing machine, in 1949. Hence the rink vehicle's name.

Across

1. HOF ind. 2016, (RW) Sergei Mak___ (Rus)
5. EA Sports NHL makers, studio is in Burnaby British Colu___
9. Pavel "Russian Rocket" Bure characteristic
13. Package of 12 pucks
14. Crowd sings ___ to anthem
16. ___sts make EA Sports NHL look good
17. Satellite equipment to watch games
18. Arena hotdogs ___ great
19. Sharks G James Reimer NN Optimus what?
20. Player(s) may be, off waivers
22. 1999 Rocket Richard Trophy, 47g, ANA
24. Multiple 12 packs of pucks
26. Sharks G James Reimer NN = Magic Angel "R" from Winnipeg
27. Crowned champs, "recently" AKA
30. Sharks G James Reimer NN
32. Flyers G Martin "___" Jones (NN)
34. Company messages in arena (short)
35. NHL Panthers C #27 "E" Luostarinen
39. NHL Stars D #23 "E" Lindell
40. Puck face shape
43. 80's great - "Michael Allen Ramsey"
44. NA Ice Rinks, 200 ft "L" x 85ft wide
46. "Accepted" the contract terms
47. Feb 7, 1876's special day for Hockey "puck"
49. NHL Kings RW #34 "A" Kaliyev
52. Ducks ECHL Affl. "T" OK Oilers
53. NHL Blackhawks D #82 "C" Jones
55. 1980s EDM Oilers owner "P" Pocklington
57. NHL Flyers C #71 Max "W"
59. Fan feeling toward rival team
63. Hockey HOF ind. 2020, (RW) Jarome Ig___
64. NHL Bruins G #35 Ullmark
66. Andrew C___ano, 2009 All-Star Fastest Skater
67. Ticket checker light-gun action
68. Flame Milan Lucic NN
69. Teams "cut" players, like it's done to a herd
70. CHL = ___inental Hockey League
71. Hockey HOF ind. 1973, (D) Doug Ha___
72. Back part of hockey skate

Down

1. CBJ, "electric" band heard after goals
2. Early NHL pros travelled by?
3. HOF ind. 2020, (RW) Marián H___ (Slo)
4. Takes you to the game
5. They get your additional hockey tickets
6. Saskatoon's WHL hockey team
7. NHL 2K VG on Apple devices, software
8. Rangers share "New York" w NFL Gi___
9. NHL Flyers LW #86 Joel "F"
10. CGY Saddledome went through one in '94
11. "Time" playing/coaching in the NHL
12. Aging player's enemy, Father what?
15. NHL Devils D #55 Mason "G"
21. Municipal option for ceremonial puck drop
23. NHL Islanders GM, "L" Lamoriello
25. Ret. G Kirk McLean play style
27. Ducks share Anaheim w MLB A___s
28. Stanley Cup awarded, end of playoff s___n
29. 1977 'Slap Shot' movie star Paul Ne___
31. Engravers will, w names onto Stanley Cup
33. Kings = hockey, Rams = ?
36. NHL Blue Jackets C #52 "E" Bemstrom
37. Krakens Brandon Tanev NN
38. B___ndy, an Avs primary uniform color
41. United Kingdom Hockey
42. Seen on the schedule
45. NHL Rangers Head Coach Gerard "G"
48. 1990 Adams Award Winner, WPG
50. NHL Wild C #16 "R" Pitlick
51. Wear on trading card will "R" its value
53. NHL record for Stanley Cups in a row (span.)
54. Cup awarded to top Men's Amateur Hockey team
56. 2021 (UFA) G Jeff Zatkoff
57. WHHOF = ___onsin Hockey Hall Of Fame
58. 2008 movie Slap Shot 3: The Ju___ League
60. WHL = Western Hockey Le___
61. Hockey HOF ind. 1967, (C) Neil Colv___
62. Stars GM Jim "N"
65. NHL was formed this month, 1917 (short)

PUZZLE 49

1	2	3	4		5	6	7	8			9	10	11	12
13					14				15		16			
17					18						19			
20				21				22		23				
			24				25		26					
27	28	29				30		31						
32					33		34				35	36	37	38
39				40		41				42		43		
44			45		46				47		48			
			49	50				51		52				
	53	54					55		56					
57					58		59				60	61	62
63				64		65				66			
67				68					69				
70				71					72				

Hockey Fact: Preceding the 1927-28 season, forward passes were not permitted in hockey.

Across

1. "T" Two Interactive, NHL 2K Sports VGs
5. NHL Oilers D #5 Cody "C"
9. HOF ind. 2009, (D) Brian Le___ (US)
13. Roster "max"
14. Rangers Don M___ey, 1984 All-Star MVP,
15. Fans hold out "H" for team to win Cup
16. After the anthem the game may what?
17. 80s ___endo console, w Blades of Steel VG
18. Calgary Flames Province (short)
19. 14yr Capitals G, Olaf Kolzig NN
20. HOF ind. 1950, (D) Graham Drink___
22. 15yr fr. Sen, Chris "N" AKA Neiler
23. TO Leafs = hockey, TO Jays = ___ball
24. 1943 Stanley Cup Champion Coach, DET
27. Has tickets, will part w them for $
29. HOF wanna-be
31. Season will, after the last game
32. NHL Panthers RW #74 Owen "T"
33. Leathers on goalies hand, like baseball (slang)
36. NHL Blue Jackets LW #29 Patrik "L"
37. Jumbotron AKA
39. 90's great - "Cameron Michael Neely"
40. "A stadium" for hockey AKA
41. NHL Wild goal-song, ___ ___ Crazy
45. Bruins 1st owner Adams was g___ magnate
46. Hockey HOF ind. 2012, (C) Mats Su___
48. NHL Avalanche D #8 "C" Makar
50. After the anthem the game may what?
52. NHL Rangers GM, "C" Drury
53. Penguin Greg P___, 1973 All-Star MVP,
56. Players do it on bench between shifts
57. Fans will after the game ends
58. Concession pick-me-up in a cup
59. Shawn H___ff, 2008 All-Star Fastest Skater
60. 1974 NHL All-Star MVP, Blues Garry "U"
61. Hockey HOF ind. 1973, (D) Doug Ha___

62. Hockey HOF ind. 1995, (D) Larry Robi___
63. A G___al Manager deals w trades

Down

1. Championships AKA
2. Tampa Bay Lightning arena, cap 19K
3. NHL Wild LW #97 "K" Kaprizov
4. HOF ind. 1963, (D) Jack Laviol___
5. Ret. Canes G "C.W." AKA The Warden
6. NHL Flames C #28 "E" Lindholm
7. Games = primary what? on NHL Network
8. Hockey HOF ind. 1993, (D) Guy Lapo___
9. Elite Hockey Alliance
10. NHL Predators RW #28 Eeli "T"
11. Team - player leader (short)
12. Booth announcer gear
13. Hockey HOF ind. 1963, (D) Phat Wi___
21. P.E.D. use in NHL was "R" at one time
23. NHL Oilers LW #16 Tyler "B"
25. Fr NYI G Rick DiPietro NN
26. NHL Senators D #98 Victor "M"
28. In the middle of the Bruins 8-spoke wheel
30. Edmonton Oilers NN
33. NHL pre WHA = ___ poly on hockey talent
34. Not playing, status
35. Senators Canadian "T" Centre, cap 19K
37. Legend Jaromir Jagr NN
38. 1994 Presidents' Trophy Winner, 112pts
39. 1994 NYR w Cup visited this President
42. LAK '09 1st rd pick, 5th overall Brayden "S"
43. Arena car hold AKA
44. Hockey HOF ind. 1967, (RW) Harry "O"
47. Fr. player & Head Coach "D" Dan Bylsma
49. Canucks Brock Bo___, 2018 All-Star MVP
51. Hockey HOF ind. 1963, (D) Harry Cam___
52. Hockey puzzle book has many a ___
54. AHL Laval Rocket on the scoreboard
55. SS Banner, 2nd word

PUZZLE 50

PUZZLE 1

S	N	E	T		A	S	S	T		A	L	L	E	N
U	T	A	H		T	H	E	O		B	O	O	N	E
B	I	K	E		T	O	N	Y		L	O	S	E	S
S	C	A	M	M	E	R	S		P	A	P	E	R	S
		O	N	E	E	Y	E	D						
A	C	H	I	L	D		A	S	E	A	S	O	N	
H	O	U	N	D		T	A	N	K		A	L	L	I
A	R	M	S		H	O	R	N	Y		R	A	L	L
N	E	A	T		A	N	T	I		C	O	T	I	A
D	Y	N	A	S	T	Y		H	A	N	S	E	N	
		L	E	O	P	A	R	D						
C	H	A	S	E	D		A	D	D	E	N	D	U	M
H	O	L	E	D		A	R	D	I		O	R	T	E
A	L	O	N	G		R	E	E	N		A	H	C	A
D	E	N	S	E		R	E	D	A		H	A	H	T

PUZZLE 2

B	U	S	H		C	A	R	L		S	E	N	K	O
O	N	T	A		O	R	C	A		E	V	A	N	S
N	I	O	R		L	M	A	N		M	A	T	E	S
G	O	N	D	O	L	A		C	H	E	L	S	E	A
O	N	E	E	Y	E	D		H	O	N				
		S	E	G	A		E	S	K	I	M	O	S	
	P	I	T	R	E		T	O	R	A	L	D		
P	O	P							I	L	L			
C	O	L	O	R	S		P	L	A	N	E			
T	R	E	T	I	A	K		T	R	I	M			
		C	L	E		R	E	N	E	W	A	L		
P	E	A	C	H	E	S		A	V	E	R	A	G	E
E	X	T	R	A		S	A	V	E		I	G	I	T
C	H	E	E	R		E	R	I	N		C	O	N	T
A	I	R	E	D		L	O	S	T		A	N	G	E

PUZZLE 3

A	H	A	B		P	A	S	T	A		T	Z	E	R
M	A	D	I		A	S	H	A	M		R	E	D	A
P	R	I	Z	E	S		A	T	E		A	R	O	G
S	T	A	N	D	S		W	A	R	R	I	O	R	S
		A	D	E	M		R	I	E	N				
C	O	N	S	I	D	E	R		C	E	S	S	O	R
E	L	I	T	E		M	E	D	A	L		L	I	E
N	L	E	Y		C	O	N	A	N		S	A	L	E
T	I	M		B	I	R	O	N		P	A	V	E	L
S	E	I	D	E	R		S	T	E	E	L	E	R	S
		O	R	C	A		E	X	T	A				
C	R	E	A	T	U	R	E		P	I	R	A	T	E
H	O	R	N		L	E	E		A	T	I	G	E	R
O	N	N	E		A	N	T	O	N		E	L	L	I
N	G	E	R		R	O	U	N	D		S	E	E	N

PUZZLE 4

W	H	A	R	R	A	M		B	A	S	I	L	
	L	I	O	N	S			R	E	N	O		
	S	E	C	O	N	D	S		H	A	T	S	
		S	E	N		R	H	A		B	E	E	
B	E	A	T	E	R		B	E	A	S	T	S	
E	L	G	I	N		E	A	R	T	H			
G	L	E	E			A	M	E	R	I	C	A	
S	I	N	G		G	U	S		N	E	T	S	
	S	T	A	N	D	U	P		K	N	O	T	
	M	E	I	E	R		P	E	T	R	O		
	B	E	A	G	L	E		K	A	R	S	O	N
S	H	A		T	I	P		P	E	R			
C	A	R	S		T	H	R	I	V	E	D		
H	I	L	A			S	H	I	N	Y			
C	R	O	W	D		S	A	N	T	E	R	I	

PUZZLE 5

	S	A	A	D			S	T	P	A	T	S	
T	H	I	N	G			P	H	A	N	E	U	F
D	I	O	N	N	E		B	A	R	R	A	S	S	O
A	G	R	E	E	S		A	S	E	K		S	P	R
N	E	T			A	R	M	E		D	I	E	D
T	R	I	A		L	I	O	S		R	E	E	N
E	S	E	R		T	H	N		A	C	A	R	D
		R	E	E	L		D	U	L	L	
	S	P	E	A	R		P	O	T		E	R	T	S
	C	A	S	T		N	E	M	O		R	E	E	T
E	A	S	T		P	E	T	E			F	E	E
T	M	S		L	O	W	E		C	L	A	U	D	E
A	M	A	R	I	N	E	R		H	A	N	S	E	N
L	E	G	E	N	D	S		E	N	T	E	R
	R	E	P	E	A	T		F	E	E	D

PUZZLE 6

	T	A	B	A	S	C	O		L	A	S	T	
S	A	T		G	O	L	F		A	N	O	V	
P	R	I	C	E	L	E	S	S		V	E	R	S
U	G	G	E		D	A	T	A		I	N	T	E	R
D	E	E	R			N	E	T			T	A	R	A
S	T	R	E	A	M		E	A	T	S		B	I	D
		A	R	O		L	N	A	H		L	E	E
	E	H	L	E	R	S		S	T	A	T	E	S
A	N	A		N	A	T	O		A	R	H	
L	T	M		O	N	O	V		R	E	E	M	E	R
E	R	I	K		R	E	S			J	I	V	E
S	A	L	E	S		E	R	A	S		O	M	A	N
	N	T	H	A		D	A	L	E	W	E	I	S	E
T	O	O	L			L	E	A	D		C	O	W
S	N	E	T			L	I	N	G	T	O	N

PUZZLE 7

S	C	O	T	T			S	P	O	R	T	S	
T	A	N	E	V		C	O	C	A		E	R	A	L
R	E	E	N			O	V	E	R		S	A	T	U
A	S	E	A	L		N	I	N	E		T	I	A	K
W	A	Y	N	E		T	E	E	N		O	N	N	E
	R	E	T	I	R	E		S	T	O	R	E	S
	S	D		P	O	S	T		P	E	D	
		O	N	T	O	I	C	E	
	C	P	L		P	L	A	N		S	O
H	E	A	D	U	P		I	C	E	M	E	N
H	U	N	T		P	U	C	K		R	I	N	E	R
A	N	T	E		G	L	E	E		S	T	A	G	E
N	G	E	R		A	L	L	I		E	T	A	L
K	U	N	Y		M	E	L	T		A	R	O	M	A
	P	E	N	N	E	D		C	A	R	E	Y

PUZZLE 8

B	E	A	M		M	I	N	T	S		T	A	P	S
O	S	S	A		A	L	E	R	T		A	S	S	O
O	P	E	N	E	R		W	A	R		N	S	O	N
K	O	N	A	M	I		S	C	A	N	N	I	N	G
		G	E	A	R		E	L	L	E	
I	N	T	E	R	N	E	T		M	A	R	C	U	S
C	A	R	R	Y		N	I	L	A	N		O	N	T
I	N	E	S		L	O	G	A	N		O	N	T	A
A	N	A		R	O	S	E	Y		T	R	A	I	N
L	E	T	A	N	G		R	E	S	I	G	N	E	D
	P	A	I	D		R	A	M	A	
A	T	L	A	N	T	I	C		T	E	N	A	N	T
C	O	O	P		E	L	H		A	R	I	V	A	L
C	U	S	E		C	L	O	W	N		Z	A	T	A
L	T	E	R		H	Y	N	E	S		E	R	O	N

PUZZLE 9 — PUZZLE 10

PUZZLE 9

```
A V C O   O J H L   B E S T
M E A N   R E N O S   O M H A
P O S T   G N A S H   T A I N
S H E A H A N   S O R T I N G
        R E N E W   W A L L Y
C O T I A   R E D E Y E
A B S O R B   A I R   S E N D
T L O   T R A P P E R   A C E
S E N S   A R O   D U N K I N
    L O S I N G   L E A S T
  C R A S H   S A B E S
C O A C H E S   R U S S E L L
R I N K   A S T A R   M E M O
E N G E   R E I G N   A L A N
E S E R   L M E S   N I N G
```

PUZZLE 10

```
C A L E   H A B S   R A G S
S A R O S   O R E E   F I A T
L U R C H   F O R M   A R T I
A S E A L   M A G I C   P   C
P E S T   C A R D   H A L A K
  S T E F A N   O P E R A T E
        O L N   G A R T N E R
  T H I R D   L I N E S
S T A R T E R   P A S
L E M A I R E   A C H I L D
E L I T E   S I T E   T I E R
D   L   S P E N T   R U T T A
D A T A   O R T E   O N T A P
O R O V   O V E R   D E L I S
G O N G   H E R N   A S E N
```

PUZZLE 11 — PUZZLE 12

PUZZLE 11

```
O R D A   U B O V   M A M I N
F O O L   P O L E   C H I C O
F A M E   G O D S   C A K E S
E R I C D A Z E   A R C A D E
      A M E R I C A
A C T I V E   C A E S A R S
S L I C E   P A I R   K L A H
H O M A   S A L A D   J A N I
A S E N   H I L L   R E I G N
M E D S T A R   G A I N E Y
      U P S T A R T
R E T I R E   W R I T E O F F
E L L E R   B E T T   A R E A
A T A R I   F E I T   R E L L
L I N E S   S T N Y   S E L L
```

PUZZLE 12

```
W T H A   S W A G   S T O N E
I R O N   T A G E   E L L I S
R E D A   E T E R   L A I N E
E N G R A V E   A R A N G E R
S T E E G E R   R O N
      N E N Y   D A N E Y K O
  C B A S S   R E P E A T
R O R         A L T
B L A C K S   C O B R A
B U D D I E S   T A P E
      S A T   O P E R A T E
L E T E S T U   L I N G T O N
A T A R I   A B E T   D O W D
B A R O N   R O D A   O R E E
S L A N G   T O O L   G O L D
```

PUZZLE 13

```
R E A M   M I N T S   B E A N
O S S A   A L F R T   A I I I
O P E N E R   T A R   N T O N
K O N A M I   S C A N N I N G
      G E A R   E L L E
I N T E R N E T   M A R C U S
C A R R Y   N I L A N   O N T
I N E S   L O G A N   O N T A
A N A   R O S E Y   T R A I N
L E T A N G   R E S I G N E D
      P A I D   R A M A
A T L A N T I C   T E N A N T
B O O P   E L H   A R I V A L
E R N E   C L O W N   Z A T A
E N E R   H Y N E S   E R O N
```

PUZZLE 14

```
W A R R O O M     M A X I M
    H A U L A       C R E E
    A K N I G H T   M A R T
      E C S   A R T   Y E S
W A F F L E   S T A I R S
R U R A L   P R I M E
A T E S     R E L E A S E
P O S T   M I D   R O L I
S H E A H A N   D U L L
  S P E N T   M O N E Y
  S T P A T S   B O N D R A
S A W   S D L   M A D
C R E D   S E C U R E D
H E A D     S T O R Y
C A R B S   J A N N E Y
```

PUZZLE 15

```
  F L I P   S H O R T Y
  M A I N E   H O N O R E D
L I S T E N   B O U D R E A U
O T T E R S   L U R E   A R M
G E E     C A T S   S T O P
O R S B   B U C S   B E E N
S A T U   R J K   P R I D E
    Y O Y O   P A I D
  S P E Z Z   J U G   E M M Y
  T O R O   P O L E   R A C E
M A U S   A I H L     G C A
A R T   A R C A   S T A I R S
S T I L L M A N   T O M C A T
S E N A T O R   A N A M E
  R E G A R D   R Y N O
```

PUZZLE 16

```
  C E N T R A L     A P A N
B A D   M I C E   L A G E
E R I C S T A A L   M I R O
A L T A   A R G A   A R E N T
K O O N   D U B   S E L L
S T R A P S   E A K A   S E E
    D A L   S N E T   T O R
  S L A T E R   C A R S O N
E H A   I G O R   T I E
L A P   O R C O   S P A S M S
K R I S   K A M   S T A T
S P E N T   E R I K   O R N E
  I R A T   M I N U S N I N E
E R K O   N O N E   K E N
S E E N   G R I N D E R
```

PUZZLE 17   PUZZLE 18

Puzzle 17

B	R	I	T		A	R	T	S		S	C	O	T	T
O	Y	E	R		M	E	T	E		P	A	R	E	E
B	A	R	A	B	A	N	O	V		A	S	E	A	L
O	N	E	F	O	R	O	N	E		T	H	E	M	E
		F	R	I		N	N	U	M					
	F	R	I	E	N	D	S		C	L	A	U	D	E
E	R	I	C		E	R	A	L		A	N	N	O	Y
R	O	N		R	O	B	O	T		T	O	T		
A	N	N	U	M		P	E	T	E		M	I	R	O
S	T	E	P	A	N		S	E	L	F	I	E	S	
		D	R	O	S		E	A	T					
T	O	T	A	L		E	R	I	C	S	T	A	A	L
A	N	T	T	I		D	O	N	A	T	E	L	L	O
S	T	E	E	N		I	L	L	S		N	T	O	N
N	O	R	D	S		N	E	A	T		S	A	N	G

Puzzle 18

F	I	L	M		D	U	M	B	A		R	A	T	E
O	N	T	A		E	V	E	R	S		E	R	T	S
W	E	E	G	A	R		S	A	T		T	I	A	K
L	Y	R	I	C	S		S	T	I	T	I	O	N	S
		C	T	O	P		T	N	E	R				
L	A	R	I	O	N	O	V		G	R	E	A	S	E
A	R	O	A	R		L	I	V	E	S		R	H	L
B	E	A	N		W	A	G	E	R		N	E	A	L
E	N	D		J	A	R	O	S		R	I	N	N	E
L	O	S	S	E	S		R	E	G	I	S	T	E	R
		E	E	T	U		Y	A	N	K				
C	O	N	C	R	E	T	E		R	E	A	V	E	S
U	S	I	O		B	I	D		A	R	N	O	T	T
P	S	O	N		I	C	I	N	G		E	U	R	O
S	A	N	D		N	A	N	N	E		N	S	O	N

PUZZLE 19   PUZZLE 20

Puzzle 19

C	O	S	T		S	W	A	P		P	A	S	S
H	O	L	E		P	A	L	A	T		I	N	T	E
O	P	E	N		O	L	L	I	E		S	T	A	N
N	E	W	Y	O	R	K		R	A	P	T	O	R	S
		E	N	T	E	R		L	I	O	N	S		
T	R	E	A	T		R	O	T	T	E	N			
M	U	R	R	A	Y		L	I	E		S	A	M	E
A	L	T		P	O	O	L	M	A	N		D	A	Y
N	E	S	S		U	N	I		M	O	B	I	L	E
	P	A	R	E	N	T		L	E	A	E	S		
	F	R	O	T	H		S	O	L	A	R			
S	L	A	N	T	E	D		W	I	N	N	I	N	G
H	A	T	S		A	R	T	E	M		I	E	D	E
U	S	I	O		D	O	U	L	I		E	R	I	N
T	H	O	R		P	E	S	T		R	E	N	O

Puzzle 20

B	A	C	C	A		O	R	C	O		M	A	Y	A
	C	O	S	T		F	O	O	D		A	C	D	C
A	N	T	O	N		E	D	O	R		O	P	E	R
R	O	A	R	S		G	E	N	E	S		T		T
B	O	N	E		H	E	R	N		L	E	A	V	E
	K	E	S	S	E	L		O	L	I	V	I	E	R
		T	I	E		R	A	C	I	N	E			
	B	A	R	O	N		R	I	N	K	S			
D	E	S	I	R	E	D		C	M	N				
A	N	T	O	I	N	E		R	E	G	A	R	D	
R	N	A	T	E		T	H	O	R		M	E	A	L
N		D		S	A	R	O	S		Y	A	N	N	I
E	R	I	K		I	O	N	S		A	L	A	I	N
L	O	U	D		R	I	D	E		S	I	M	E	K
L	Y	M	P		S	T	A	D		H	E	E	L

PUZZLE 21　PUZZLE 22

```
PUZZLE 21
A C A P   R A D E   R A N G E
M E A U   E R I N   E L I A S
P Ü H L   P Ü Ö L   D A N T E
B I L L F O L D   C E N T E R
        F R E E W A Y
O F F S E T   O N E T I M E
F O O T Y   W O M E   A M A N
F O R E   B A T E S   P A N D
E T T E   A R T N   S E G G Y
R E Y N A R D   V I D E O S
        B R O S H I E
R E I L L Y   H E N R I Q U E
O R A M A   M E A N   M U R R
N A M E D   A R D I   B A R N
C L O S E   D O S E   E R I E
```

```
PUZZLE 22
D I S C   C O R D   M E D A L
I S T O   A K F R   A R O M A
S P A N   N E D Y   G O M E Z
C E N T E N E   D E N N E N Y
O R D E R O F   E R A
        S I T E   N A T U R A L
        O A T E S   S E V E R E
J O E             T E D
C E R N A K   P L A Z A
L E O N S I S   T R O M
        E N L   R E N E W A L
S T O R A G E   A V E R A G E
C A N E S   D A V E   I G I T
A R E N O   G L I N   C O N T
M A S O N   E A S T   A N G E
```

PUZZLE 23　PUZZLE 24

```
PUZZLE 23
A S T R   S C A M S   M I R O
I E R E   C O M I C   C R A N
R A I D E R   E L H   C A D E
S T A B L E   N A R R A T E S
        A G E S   N I O N
A M A R I N E R   N A N A N A
D A M O N   D U P E R   G I N
U T I N   O I L E R   M E E T
L E G   G E N E S   P I N T O
T R A D E S   S C R A N T O N
        R A T E   E E L I
V E N D R E D I   M A S C O T
O W E R   R G S   O T T A W A
V I T A   L E A S T   E V E N
A S S I   E S C H E   R E N T
```

```
PUZZLE 24
R I C H A R D     T E M P T
    B A C O N     S I E R
    A N T O S K I   A C C O
        D O T   A R M   H A M
D A G G E R   G I V A N I
A W A R D   A L I K E
T I T A   R E N E W A L
A N O N   M T R   S H E Y
G R A T T O N   M A T E
    T H E M E   R A N T A
    B O E S E R   R E N D E R
A T J   M T N   S A D
C T O P   S T A N D U P
H A R M   L E A C H
A N K L E   S T R E A M S
```

PUZZLE 25   PUZZLE 26

Puzzle 25	Puzzle 26
PENN STRAWS	BLABBER SKIN
MILAN THERIEN	FEE EEMU HANA
JAROME PERSONAL	OFTHEEAST UNCR
ARACER REET NBA	LOTE FISH TERRY
DIT TAGE BEAN	DREW LIE READ
ENEG ANTS TERS	SERIAL ACAP ATE
NOSE JET CHESS	TWO NADA SON
RBER SAUK	ARTIST NUTTER
LIMIT BAD ERTS	AGE NEIL LCR
ALAN DOME REAL	BEL GREE THECAT
ANON PILE ALA	ONOP DOS NENY
RCV JOST BRADEN	RECAP UPTO INCL
THEGUINS RISING	RATS PARDONTHE
SELANNE AGENT	ATIO RAGH ROR
SAFETY DING	LEON DWELLER

PUZZLE 27   PUZZLE 28

Puzzle 27	Puzzle 28
TIRE SNAP TOMAS	SPUR SPOON MAMA
EVAL ACCL ANAME	OORE CARRY CLAP
METALLICA VEGAN	FORMER CAL GATE
PRESEASON AGENT	TRIPLE AMARINER
TOR EURO	AVEL ANON
JOINING SEATID	SCHRINER DANISH
RONC EELI SLICE	THATS WATER RHA
ANA SCOTT MIL	ROSS LINER SWAG
PAIRS KACH RENZ	AKA WASTE STING
SHRIMP THEFARG	PENNER ATTORNEY
BIKE BAD	EATT HILA
CODER NUMERICAL	SALARIES CALLER
ALAIN DREAMCAST	ERAL SAT ARMADA
MICRO ERTS AGLE	AINE TRENT ADDS
OSHOV DIET LEUR	TNER ESPYS NDYK

PUZZLE 29   PUZZLE 30

```
PUZZLE 29
A D I A   S A L E     F A S T
M O L D   T W E E T   E L L F
P O L I   E A G L E   R E A L
B R E A K E R   I A F R A T E
      B A N D S   L E A F S
F I E L D   S L A T E R
A B S O R B   A G E   O N O V
C L E   I R O N M A N   A R O
T E R S   A T T   M A P L E S
      M A S T E R   M A L E S
  F E A T S   D A T E S
B O X S E A T   N E S S M A N
O R T H   R E N O S   A E R O
A C R E   D E B U T   G L E E
T E A D     N A T S   E T A L
```

```
PUZZLE 30
A N O N   M O S T   T A R A
G R A P E   E A C H   A O J I
L I N E S   E T R O   B E S T
E V A N S   T E A R S   N   K
D A N E   L I S T   T E A S E
  L A R S E N   C L A Y T O N
        E G G   H O R T O N
  S I N C E   S T O R Y
P I S T O N S   S E E
L A L O N D E   A R R E S T
A H A N D   M O N S   B A R N
Y   N   S H E L F   L E V E L
O A D R   E N D O   V R A N A
F R E E   A K E R   E L G I N
F O R M   L O R D   S E E N
```

PUZZLE 31   PUZZLE 32

```
PUZZLE 31
C A N A   I L M O   B A T E S
A B E R   N E O N   A N A M E
R E A M   F A T E   S T A I N
T E L E C A S T   S K I L L S
      O N T O I C E
C H A B O T   C A T F I S H
H A S E K   B E A M   O R P I
A G E L   P E N N S   O V E N
R E A L   R A L S   S T I N T
A L L S T A R   G U E N T Z
      I N S T E A D
A B L O C K   E X I S T I N G
C L I C K   B A I N   A V E L
C O O K E   O R T E   P I L E
O W N E R   O S S Y   E L L E
```

```
PUZZLE 32
O R P I   L N A H   P L E T T
R O A R   E I H A   R I N N E
L O G O   G I O N   E D G E S
O P E N N E T   D E S S E R T
V E R M O N T   E Y E
      A N D Y   D E N N E N Y
  C A N E S   S T A T U E
C R P           A T S
B E A S T S   D E A L S
C E N T R A L   B E A R
      A L A   R A T T R A P
C A S H I E R   A L L T I M E
A L A I N   M A D I   U N I T
D A N T E   E M E N   R E G I
E N D E D   R O N G   I R A T
```

PUZZLE 33   PUZZLE 34

PUZZLE 33

```
A S L U   H O N D A   A H A C
U N I T   A N T O N   M I K A
T A V E R N   H U D   O V E R
O P E N E D   A L E T T E R B
    S A L E   I R A T
A C C I D E N T   S P O R T S
R A L L Y   D A T E S   O U T
T U E S   V E G A N   M O R E
E S A   F E D U N   D A N C E
M E R C E R   P E D E R S O N
  H I S S   V E N S
L E P E T I T E   A S H A R K
O R E E   O R R   L E A D I N
N A T S   N A N N E   L I N E
G L E E   S W E A R   L A K E
```

PUZZLE 34

```
W A R R O O M   I S S E L
  H A U L A   A E R O
  A K N I G H T   T A N S
  E C S   A R R   B E E
W A F F L E   S T A I R S
R U R A L   P R I Z E
A T E S   R E L E A S E
P O S T   M I D   R O L I
  S H E A H A N   D U L L
  S P E N T   H O N E Y
  S T P A T S   B O N D R A
S A P   S D L   M I L
C R E D   S E C O N D S
H E A D   A R G U E
C A R B S   L E O P A R D
```

PUZZLE 35   PUZZLE 36

PUZZLE 35

```
  C A H A   C H E A T S
  D O L A N   H E R S H E Y
R A N K I N   D E A N G E L O
E N T I R E   I E D E   K A Y
A I R   L O S S   M O N O
V E O H   R I D E   G I O N
O L L E   A C E   R I N N E
  I N L A   S A N D
C A N E S   P E D   E R T S
O N E S   B A N E   R E E T
A M A N   W E S T   F E E
S P R   H E A T   C L A U D E
T H E C O B R A   H A N S E N
R E N A M E D   E N T E R
R A C E R S   F E E D
```

PUZZLE 36

```
  C E N T R A L   S A B S
B A D   M I C E   H E A T
E R I C S T A A L   A R R I
A L T A   A R G A   W O R L D
K O O N   D U B   S A L O
S T R A P S   E A K A   S M W
  D A L   S N E T   S A D
  S L A T E R   C A R S O N
E H A   I G O R   T I E
S A P   O R C O   S P A S M S
K R I S   K A M   S T A T
S P E N T   E R I K   O R N E
  I R A T   M I N U S N I N E
E R K O   N O N E   P E N
S E E N   G R I N D E R
```

PUZZLE 37   PUZZLE 38

```
PUZZLE 37
C O N S  ·  L M A N  ·  K N I F E
L O N E  ·  L I N E  ·  E A C L E
I R O N R A N G E  ·  S T A A L
P E R S O N N E L  ·  S U N N Y
   F A D  ·  Y N E R  ·
  A N A R E N A  ·  V L A D A R
I R O N  ·  R E L O  ·  S L U G S
D O S  ·  S L A N G  ·  P R O  ·
S M E L L  ·  L I T E  ·  T E E N
T A K E I N  ·  N O S C O R E  ·
   T B O T  ·  T O M  ·
L E T T E  ·  A C R U S A D E R
E L L E R  ·  S H O R T L I N E
A L E R T  ·  T E L E  ·  E S K S
D E R B Y  ·  E W I S  ·  S H O T
```

```
PUZZLE 38
A H A B  ·  P O L A R  ·  A S S I
M A D I  ·  A N A M E  ·  D O O R
P R I Z E S  ·  C O W  ·  J D U B
S T A N D S  ·  E V A L U A T E
  A D E M  ·  E R T S  ·
C O N S I D E R  ·  D E T A C H
E L I T E  ·  D U P E R  ·  C H A
N L E Y  ·  S A L A D  ·  P L A T
T I M  ·  T Y L E R  ·  W E I S E
S E I D E R  ·  S T R A P P E D
  R E A D  ·  S E T S  ·
F I N A N C E S  ·  N E I L E R
O L I G  ·  U B S  ·  A R C A D E
R Y N O  ·  S T O R M  ·  A N D A
M A G N  ·  E S C H E  ·  N D Y K
```

PUZZLE 39   PUZZLE 40

```
PUZZLE 39
H O M A  ·  I C H T  ·  S A A D
E N E R  ·  S H O U T  ·  E L L E
I N L A  ·  P A T C H  ·  A L E S
R E T I R E S  ·  H E R B E R T
  D I R E C  ·  C H A N T
T A N E V  ·  D U B O I S  ·
O U T R A G  ·  B E B  ·  S O F A
M S H  ·  L O M B E R G  ·  W I N
S T A T  ·  O V I  ·  A R R E S T
  H O S T E D  ·  E A R T H
  S T I L E  ·  S E V E N
O P E N N E T  ·  F I N G E R S
R E A K  ·  G O M E R  ·  E R O N
C A S E  ·  G R A N T  ·  R I D E
A K E R  ·  O D D S  ·  S E A T
```

```
PUZZLE 40
  C H A T  ·  L A K E  ·  A G E S
S O U T H  ·  E R A L  ·  N E A T
P I N T O  ·  C O L L  ·  A N T E
U N G E R  ·  L A Y E R  ·  E  ·  C
R E E N  ·  B A R N  ·  E A R T H
  D R D R A I  ·  U P S C A L E
    O R R  ·  K O P I T A R
  A R M O R  ·  D E F E N
T W E A K E D  ·  S E C  ·
H O S T I L E  ·  M I T E R A
E L I T E  ·  A P A N  ·  B E S T
P  ·  G  ·  S A L E S  ·  W E I S E
H A N D  ·  D I S H  ·  A R M I A
I L E Y  ·  I N C E  ·  S L E G R
L A D E  ·  A G E D  ·  H E R N
```

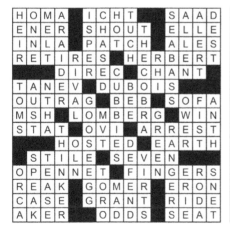

PUZZLE 41

A	D	A	M		E	L	L	S		S	T	R	A	W
V	O	T	E		K	E	E	P		A	U	D	I	O
A	R	E	A		N	A	T	S		F	R	O	D	O
R	E	S	T	R	I	C	T		P	E	N	N	E	D
				O	N	H	E	A	R	T				
B	A	T	T	L	E		R	E	Y	N	A	R	D	
A	S	E	A	L		C	R	E	D		O	H	I	O
C	H	A	Z		R	O	O	N	S		L	A	N	Z
C	A	S	E		O	N	T	A		J	A	N	N	E
A	M	E	R	I	C	A		S	I	N	D	E	N	
			C	E	N	T	R	A	L					
O	P	E	N	E	R		R	O	L	L	B	A	C	K
R	A	D	I	M		C	O	C	O		A	P	A	N
S	P	O	K	E		R	I	C	O		N	O	T	E
B	A	R	O	N		P	S	O	N		G	L	E	E

PUZZLE 42

S	Y	R	A		K	O	N	T		S	T	A	T	E
T	A	A	L		E	L	F	O		T	O	T	A	L
A	C	C	L		N	E	L	L		A	R	E	N	T
T	H	E	T	A	N	K		E	D	R	O	S	K	I
S	T	R	I	P	E	S		D	O	T				
			M	E	D	Y		O	N	E	G	A	M	E
E	W	E	R	Y				T	R	A	D	E	D	
A	X	E									A	T	M	
S	T	A	Y	A	T			B	L	A	M	E		
G	A	R	T	N	E	R		H	E	I	R			
			T	L	O		R	A	T	T	R	A	P	
H	A	T	C	H	E	T		O	N	E	T	I	M	E
I	D	A	H	O		A	I	N	E		U	N	I	T
N	I	L	A	N		T	L	E	R		R	E	G	I
S	A	L	T	Y		E	L	K	S		I	R	A	T

PUZZLE 43

A	N	T	S		R	O	M	A	N		W	A	R	E
M	A	R	Y		A	T	A	R	I		A	G	E	L
P	H	I	L	L	Y		R	G	S		R	E	A	L
S	L	A	V	I	N		T	O	K	A	R	S	K	I
			A	V	E	R		S	A	V	E			
A	G	E	N	E	R	A	L		N	A	N	A	N	A
B	L	A	I	S		D	U	P	E	R		G	I	N
O	O	G	A		T	A	P	I	N		M	E	E	T
L	V	L		T	H	R	E	E		P	I	N	T	O
T	E	E	D	E	R		S	C	R	A	N	T	O	N
			B	E	E	P		E	E	L	I			
R	E	D	A	L	E	R	T		P	A	S	S	E	D
E	R	I	C		W	I	I		O	T	T	E	R	S
L	I	N	K		A	S	T	A	R		E	N	K	O
L	E	G	S		Y	E	A	S	T		R	S	O	N

PUZZLE 44

H	A	R	D	E	S	T		L	U	P	E	S
	R	E	N	E	W			S	E	T	O	
	C	A	N	N	O	N	S		E	S	E	R
		L	I	D		O	H	A		K	M	T
S	O	U	L	E	S		A	G	E	N	C	Y
E	N	T	E	R		N	O	R	T	H		
L	A	I	M		T	O	O	H	I	G	H	
L	I	C	A		G	O	D		L	L	E	D
R	A	I	L	E	R	S		L	E	N	O	
	R	A	D	E	K		S	E	N	K	O	
	S	E	R	G	E	I		M	A	R	N	E	R
P	R	O		S	E	N		B	I	D		
O	O	R	E		S	E	C	O	N	D	S	
T	O	R	N			A	D	U	L	T		
S	T	Y	L	E		L	Y	S	E	L	L	

PUZZLE 45 PUZZLE 46

PUZZLE 45

	H	A	T	S			A	B	L	O	C	K	
	C	A	U	S	E		M	A	N	N	E	R	S
D	A	N	T	O	N		L	O	C	A	T	I	O	N
O	N	I	O	N	S		E	T	C	H		L	E	E
M	A	F			Z	A	T	A			L	I	N	K
E	D	I	T		T	A	C	O		D	A	N	K
D	A	N	O		A	R	H		L	A	R	G	E
		R	P	H	Y		P	A	L	M			
	O	R	A	M	A		W	E	D		E	R	A	S
	C	E	L	L		G	O	N	E		R	I	C	H
T	O	D	D		G	A	R	S			C	H	I
E	N	L		E	A	T	L		N	A	P	K	I	N
A	N	I	M	A	T	E	D		C	H	E	L	L	Y
D	O	N	S	K	O	I		H	A	T	E	D
	R	E	G	A	R	D		A	C	E	S

PUZZLE 46

	H	A	R	D	E	S	T		A	S	S	T
I	O	S		W	L	P	H		A	H	C	A
N	O	S	E	B	L	E	E	D		H	A	H	T
S	P	I	N		S	A	M	E		A	R	M	I	A
T	E	S	T		K	A	M			P	A	C	K
A	R	T	I	S	T		L	E	F	T		L	E	E
			A	I	R		L	L	O	W		T	K	N
	M	C	L	E	A	N		O	L	E	S	Z
L	O	U		V	I	E	L		D	E	C
I	N	L		E	L	L	E		S	T	U	M	P	Y
A	S	T	R			S	A	D			D	A	H	O
S	T	U	N	T		O	F	O	Z		S	L	O	T
	E	R	A	L		N	I	N	E	T	Y	O	N	E
	R	A	T	E		E	U	R	O		N	E	S
	S	L	E	Y		S	T	O	R	I	E	S

PUZZLE 47 PUZZLE 48

PUZZLE 47

S	C	O	T	T			D	B	A	C	K	S
T	A	N	E	V		S	T	A	R		H	O	T	N
R	E	E	N		E	E	L	I		I	V	A	N
A	S	E	A	L		I	L	L	E		M	A	Y	O
W	A	Y	N	E		B	E	A	R		E	L	A	N
	R	E	T	I	R	E		S	E	C	R	E	T
	S	D		P	O	R	T		A	A	V
			O	C	T	O	P	U	S
		C	A	L		T	A	N	S		M	A
	H	O	L	D	U	P		T	I	E	D	U	P
C	A	R	B		P	E	S	T		L	I	M	I	T
A	N	N	E		G	R	E	E		S	A	B	R	E
N	G	E	R		A	M	E	R			B	L	A	S
A	U	L	T		M	I	N	N		F	L	E	T	T
P	L	A	N	E	T			L	O	S	E	S

PUZZLE 48

L	E	A	D		S	C	R	A	P		S	H	E	A
I	E	R	E		T	H	E	M	E		P	A	R	M
O	T	T	A	W	A		C	O	P		O	R	N	E
S	U	N	D	A	Y		C	U	S	T	O	M	E	R
			L	I	A	S		R	I	E	N
A	R	T	I	S	T	I	C		C	A	S	S	I	E
S	A	I	N	T		T	O	T	A	L		P	M	L
E	N	G	E		F	E	D	U	N		M	E	A	L
A	T	E		L	O	S	E	R		R	A	N	G	E
L	A	R	M	E	R		R	E	P	O	R	T	E	R
		A	G	E	S		K	O	V	I
H	A	N	D	I	C	A	P		C	E	N	T	E	R
I	P	O	D		A	L	A		K	R	E	U	T	Y
D	A	N	O		S	E	N	S	E		R	N	A	N
E	N	E	G		T	I	G	H	T		S	A	L	O

PUZZLE 49   PUZZLE 50

PUZZLE 49

A	R	O	V		M	B	I	A			F	A	S	T
C	A	S	E		A	L	O	N	G		A	R	T	I
D	I	S	H		T	A	S	T	E		R	E	I	M
C	L	A	I	M	E	D		S	E	L	A	N	N	E
			C	A	S	E	S		R	O	B	O	T	
N	E	W	L	Y		S	T	A	T	U	E			
G	A	M	E	O	F		A	D	S		E	E	T	U
E	S	A		R	O	U	N	D	E	D		M	A	R
L	O	N	G		O	K	D		N	A	M	I	N	G
		A	R	T	H	U	R		T	U	L	S	A	
	C	A	L	E	B		P	E	T	E	R			
W	I	L	L	M	A	N		D	I	S	D	A	I	N
I	N	L	A		L	I	N	U	S		O	G	L	I
S	C	A	N		L	O	O	C	H		C	U	L	L
C	O	N	T			R	V	E	Y		H	E	E	L

PUZZLE 50

T	A	K	E		C	E	C	I		E	T	C	H
L	I	M	I	T		A	L	O	N		H	O	P	E
S	T	A	R	T		N	I	N	T		A	L	T	A
O	L	L	I	E		W	A	T	E	R		V		D
N	E	I	L		B	A	S	E		A	D	A	M	S
	S	E	L	L	E	R		N	O	M	I	N	E	E
			E	N	D		T	I	P	P	E	T	T	
M	I	T	T	S			L	A	I	N	E			
M	O	N	I	T	O	R		C	M	N				
A	N	A	R	E	N	A		L	E	T	S	G	O	
R	O	C	E	R		N	D	I	N		C	A	L	E
I		T		B	E	G	I	N		C	H	R	I	S
O	L	I	S		R	E	S	T		L	E	A	V	E
J	A	V	A		O	R	C	O		U	N	G	E	R
R	V	E	Y		N	S	O	N		E	N	E	R	

116

CONGRATULATIONS
YOU FINISHED

DESIGNER INK – ALL AGES BOOKS
HOMESCHOOL INK – SCHOOL BOOKS
SUPER KIDZ – KIDS BOOKS

designerinkbooks@gmail.com

Quotes   Theme

Books   →   "Designer Ink" sports   🔍

Search AMAZON today! or

Type into   Amazon Standard
Amazon   ID Number

B08L3XCCMC   **B09M58P48J**   **B08P15YF7K**   **B086PTBBBW**

B089TTYR34   **B089M5Z58C**   **B085K78C6Y**   **B08PJK7CWM**

ALL SPORTS   CROSSWORD
MOVIES   WORD SEARCH
CAMPING – HIKING   SUDOKU
FISHING – HUNTING   LARGE PRINT
USA CANADA   KIDS WS
CATS – PETS   KIDS MAZES
ALL HOLIDAYS   KIDS COLORING

FB: @DESIGNERINKBOOKS

INFO SOURCE WIKIPEDIA.COM

Made in the USA
Las Vegas, NV
02 December 2024

13219990R00066